Words *of* Power,
Echoes *of* Praise

Other books by Lynnda Ell

Changing Me, Change the World, Prayers from the Psalms, Book I

Presented To:

_____

By:

_____

On:

_____

Words *of* Power, Echoes *of* Praise

*Prayers from the Psalms,
Book II*

Lynnda Ell

Copyright © 2011 Lynnda Ell

All rights reserved. No part of this book may be used or reproduced by any means, graphic, electronic, or mechanical, including photocopying, recording, taping or by any information storage retrieval system without the written permission of the publisher except in the case of brief quotations embodied in critical articles and reviews.

Scripture quotations are from The Holy Bible, English Standard Version(r) (ESV(r)), copyright (c) 2001 by Crossway, a publishing ministry of Good News Publishers. Used by permission. All rights reserved.

WestBow Press books may be ordered through booksellers or by contacting:

WestBow Press
A Division of Thomas Nelson
1663 Liberty Drive
Bloomington, IN 47403
www.westbowpress.com
1-(866) 928-1240

Because of the dynamic nature of the Internet, any web addresses or links contained in this book may have changed since publication and may no longer be valid. The views expressed in this work are solely those of the author and do not necessarily reflect the views of the publisher, and the publisher hereby disclaims any responsibility for them.

Any people depicted in stock imagery provided by Thinkstock are models, and such images are being used for illustrative purposes only.

Certain stock imagery © Thinkstock.

ISBN: 978-1-4497-2263-0 (sc)
ISBN: 978-1-4497-2264-7 (hc)
ISBN: 978-1-4497-2262-3 (e)

Library of Congress Control Number: 2011915519

Printed in the United States of America

WestBow Press rev. date: 9/2/2011

To the amazing women in my family:
Jeanita Pruitt, Melana Martin, Julie Lugar,
Cheryl Guyton, and Judy Hoormann

Contents

Acknowledgments	1
Preface	3
Psalm 42	4
Washed Ashore by Breaking Waves	5
Psalm 43	6
Send Your Light	7
Psalm 44	8
You Are My King, Oh God	9
Psalm 45	12
The Marriage Celebration	13
Psalm 46	16
City of Safety	17
Psalm 47	18
A Greater Gathering	19
Psalm 48	20
Jerusalem, City of Supernatural Peace	21
Psalm 49	24
Death Shall Be Their Shepherd	25
Psalm 50	28
Thankful Hearts	29

Psalm 51	32
Restore to Me the Treasures of Heaven	33
Psalm 52	36
The Wealth of Sand Castles	37
Psalm 53	38
Fools and Followers	39
Psalm 54	40
The Vindicator	41
Psalm 55:1–16	42
Betrayed!	43
Psalm 55:17–23	46
Shattered on a Sure Foundation	47
Psalm 56	48
I Choose to Live in Praise	49
Psalm 57	50
Storms Cannot Destroy	51
Psalm 58	52
Judge of Judges	53
Psalm 59	54
Media Frenzy	55
Psalm 60	58
Battle Strategy	59
Psalm 61	60

Graduation Day	61
Psalm 62	62
Battered by Life	63
Psalm 63	66
Living in the Land of Liars	67
Psalm 64	68
Conspiracy Schemes	69
Psalm 65	70
Crowned with Your Bounty	71
Psalm 66	74
Make His Praise Glorious	75
Psalm 67	78
A Blessing from Israel	79
Psalm 68:1–14	80
An Attack of Loneliness	81
Psalm 68:15–35	84
Victory Parade	85
Psalm 69:1–15	88
Prophet's Prayer	89
Psalm 69:16–36	92
Tough Love	93
Psalm 70	96
Panic Button	97

PSALM 71	98
WITH AGE, MY STRENGTH FAILS	99
PSALM 72	102
THE COMING KINGDOM	103
PSALM 73	106
DEAD-END WORLD	107
PSALM 74	110
RESTRAIN THE TIDES OF EVIL	111
PSALM 75	114
HUMILITY OR HUMILIATION	115
PSALM 76	116
WE ARE NOT THE JUDGE	117
PSALM 77	118
CARRY ME WHILE I CRY	119
PSALM 78:1–8	122
LIKE LINKS IN A CHAIN	123
PSALM 78:9–39	124
AS FICKLE AS THE WIND	125
PSALM 78:40–55	130
LIVING IN THE FOGGY MIDDLE	131
PSALM 78:56–66	134
PATIENT LOVE FOR WAYWARD MAN	135
PSALM 78:67–72	136

To Be Chosen	137
Psalm 79	140
Where Were You, God?	141
Psalm 80	142
The Saving Shepherd	143
Psalm 81	146
Songs of Worship	147
Psalm 82	150
The Supreme Court	151
Psalm 83	152
Your Purpose Stands	153

Acknowledgments

Dan Smythe, associate missionary with Global Training Network, was the first person to purchase *Changing Me, Change the World*. He promptly encouraged me to write book two. I wanted to focus on launching book one, so I told Dan to take it up with my Boss, which he did. Because Dan, members of my Bible study group, many of my other friends, and most of my family prayed, *Words of Power, Echoes of Praise* is here.

The prayers were critical, but no less important were the readers who kept me from making grammatical mistakes and other blunders. Many thanks to Muriel Watson, Anna Chatelaine, Brenda Tullos, Phillomena Kalosky, Janet Torres, Jean Davidson, and Betty Roberts.

Because of the generous editorial policies of Crossway publishing, psalms from the *Holy Bible, English Standard Version* are included with the prayers. Thank you, Crossway, for allowing me to use complete psalms in my books.

My son-in-law, Matt Lugar, and my friend, Tina Gaspard, gave me the photos that appear on the front and back covers. Thank you both for your marvelous gifts.

My heartfelt appreciation goes to Peter Perdue and Erin McCauley from WestBow Press. Their professional commitment to excellence and their patient encouragement of an emerging author brought book one to reality. I gladly trust WestBow Press with book two.

Most of all, I am blessed by the opportunity to share these prayers with you. Thank you for your interest in learning to pray directly from the Scriptures. I pray that your life will be echoes of praise as you pray back to God His words of power.

Preface

Most religions have some form of prayer. These prayers usually contain words that repeat in a certain way, in distinct patterns or at specific times. Repetition works the lips without necessarily involving the brain or engaging the heart. Repetitive prayer forms a habit of praying, but does not produce a relationship with God. True communication results in a real relationship.

Words of Power, Echoes of Praise contains prayers that communicate. "Words of Power" are the psalms. With the book open, these psalms always appear on the left page. The psalms contain passages about God, to God, and from God. Occasionally, the word *Selah* appears in a psalm. This word is a written pause, giving you a chance to stop and consider what you read.

The prayers are always on the right page. These are the "Echoes of Praise." As you read and reflect on the psalm, think of the ways the psalmist speaks for you in your specific circumstances. Then compare your thoughts with the prayer I wrote on the right-hand page. The written prayer may or may not connect with the prayer you want to pray, but it should inspire you to think of prayer as real conversation with God, who listens to you and responds to you.

Some psalms contain a substantial number of verses. When the psalm is lengthy, I divide it. For example, Psalm 69 has thirty-six verses. I wrote "Prophets' Prayer" for verses 1–15 and "Tough Love" for verses 16–36.

As you read *Words of Power, Echoes of Praise*, reach out and connect with God. Discover how wonderful He is.

Be blessed!

Lynnda Ell
New Orleans, LA

Psalm 42

1. As a deer pants for flowing streams, so pants my soul for you, O God.

2. My soul thirsts for God, for the living God. When shall I come and appear before God?

3. My tears have been my food day and night, while they say to me continually, "Where is your God?"

4. These things I remember, as I pour out my soul: how I would go with the throng and lead them in procession to the house of God with glad shouts and songs of praise, a multitude keeping festival.

5. Why are you cast down, O my soul, and why are you in turmoil within me? Hope in God; for I shall again praise him, my salvation

6. and my God. My soul is cast down within me; therefore I remember you from the land of Jordan and of Hermon, from Mount Mizar.

7. Deep calls to deep at the roar of your waterfalls; all your breakers and your waves have gone over me.

8. By day the Lord commands his steadfast love, and at night his song is with me, a prayer to the God of my life.

9. I say to God, my rock: "Why have you forgotten me? Why do I go mourning because of the oppression of the enemy?"

10. As with a deadly wound in my bones, my adversaries taunt me, while they say to me continually, "Where is your God?"

11. Why are you cast down, O my soul, and why are you in turmoil within me? Hope in God; for I shall again praise him, my salvation and my God.

Washed Ashore by Breaking Waves

How can this happen, Lord? I don't understand. Walking, loving, and living in Your presence fills my life with meaning. Yet now, I feel totally shut off from You. Like a deer in the middle of a drought pants for one more drink of water, I crave communion with You.

The emptiness where once I felt joy and peace breaks something inside of me. I cry day and night. I cry so much that my stomach hurts and my head throbs.

People who don't know You say, "Where is your God when you need Him? Why worship God when He abandons you?"

People from church say, "Buck up! Get a grip. Stop feeling sorry for yourself."

If only I could go to church and worship You. There I could get some relief from my distress, but even that is denied me. I have only sweet memories of former times when we gathered to worship You. These walls separate me from everyone and everything that I love.

You know the reason I am depressed, Lord. My heart is shattered. My mind is torn apart. I am completely undone. No doctor can repair my heart or heal my mind. At best, they might treat the symptoms. No, You are my only hope. If You don't heal me, I live in brokenness. That describes me, right now. I am tumbled over waterfalls, washed ashore by breaking waves.

Lord, I need to *see* the evidence of Your steadfast love. I need to *hear* songs of praise to You in the night. You are my Rock, so why do I feel so abandoned? I feel as though I have a thousand little demons whispering in my ears, "Where is your God now?" They taunt me with, "If God loved you, would He treat you like this?"

I am weary of my loneliness, Lord. I can deal with any experience as long as You hold me in Your hands. Nevertheless, I am human. I need to enjoy the experience of walking and communing with You. You have *never* failed to meet my needs, so I will continue to trust in Your mercy.

I cannot understand how my loneliness, depression, and pain are part of Your plan for my life. However—regardless of what happens—I trust You. Now and forever, I sing Your praises, waiting for You to deliver me, knowing in my deepest heart that You are with me. I cling to You.

Psalm 43

1. Vindicate me, O God, and defend my cause against an ungodly people, from the deceitful and unjust man deliver me!

2. For you are the God in whom I take refuge; why have you rejected me? Why do I go about mourning because of the oppression of the enemy?

3. Send out your light and your truth; let them lead me; let them bring me to your holy hill and to your dwelling!

4. Then I will go to the altar of God, to God my exceeding joy, and I will praise you with the lyre, O God, my God.

5. Why are you cast down, O my soul, and why are you in turmoil within me?

Send Your Light

I tremble, Lord, feeling trapped in a cave where the darkness smothers me. Vindictive, ungodly men call out advice. "Ten steps to the left takes you to safety," shouts one. "No, go back the way you came," calls another. "You're standing on the edge of a pit," whispers a third.

How do they know the way? Do the blind lead the blind, careless of the consequences? Why do I hear every voice except Yours? Have You rejected me?

My confusion paralyzes me. I am helpless to proceed in safety. Please, Lord, send Your light and show me Your way. At Your Word I will gladly take the next step even if I cannot see the path.

Your light guides me through the dangers that surround me. Your loving care and protection give me the courage to step out in faith. Every step along this perilous path brings me closer to Your dwelling, Your throne in heaven. There I will see You—my joy complete—and I will praise You forever.

This is my hope as I wait on You. I remain standing in this spot until You send Your light. I look to You to save me from this confusion and for You to instruct me in Your path. You are my light and my salvation.

Psalm 44

1. O God, we have heard with our ears, our fathers have told us, what deeds you performed in their days, in the days of old:

2. you with your own hand drove out the nations, but them you planted; you afflicted the peoples, but them you set free;

3. for not by their own sword did they win the land, nor did their own arm save them, but your right hand and your arm, and the light of your face, for you delighted in them.

4. You are my King, O God; ordain salvation for Jacob!

5. Through you we push down our foes; through your name we tread down those who rise up against us.

6. For not in my bow do I trust, nor can my sword save me.

7. But you have saved us from our foes and have put to shame those who hate us.

8. In God we have boasted continually, and we will give thanks to your name forever.

Selah

9. But you have rejected us and disgraced us and have not gone out with our armies.

10. You have made us turn back from the foe, and those who hate us have gotten spoil.

11. You have made us like sheep for slaughter and have scattered us among the nations.

12. You have sold your people for a trifle, demanding no high price for them.

YOU ARE MY KING, OH GOD

You are my King, oh God.

At home, my father and my mother taught me about You from the earliest days of my childhood. I learned about Adam and Eve in the Garden of Eden. They told me the stories of Abraham, David, and Paul. They introduced me to You, Jesus. You drew me before I was old enough to know what it meant to accept Your sacrifice on the cross as punishment for my sins.

In school, I learned about the founding of our country. You—with Your own hand—drove out the Indian nations. Though thousands died in battles that the Indians fought to protect their lands, You were the one who broke the Indian nations through the diseases that killed their people.

Why did You delight in us, to give us this mighty nation? Why did You shine the light of Your face on us when we deserved nothing? Why did You set us free from the bonds of tyranny and use Your right hand and Your arm to bless us abundantly? All I can see is that You set us in this land for purposes of Your own; certainly we did nothing to deserve this blessing.

You are my King, oh God.

Many times in history, our nation has gone to war. Through Your power, we pushed down our foes. By Your Name, we trod on those who rose up against us. When You gave us victory after victory, we exclaimed, "In God we continually boast. We will always remember what You have done for us and give You thanks." We lied. We quickly forgot Your protection. We created monuments to memorialize the ultimate sacrifice made by men and women who protected our nation. Where are the stones of remembrance that would call us to come to You in gratitude for Your divine protection? Even a simple memorial to You that was erected by survivors of World War I was destroyed by those who stand against You.

Our nation rejects You. Is it any wonder that You reject us and bring shame upon us? You no longer go out with our armies. Our foes assault us, killing us, attempting to destroy our way of life.

You are my King, oh God.

Even as the nation has turned away from You, You still have many people in this country. More and more, however, our country has no place for us. Instead, You have made us like sheep for slaughter. We are defenseless in our own culture. You have made us the taunt of our

13 You have made us the taunt of our neighbors, the derision and scorn of those around us.

14 You have made us a byword among the nations, a laughingstock among the peoples.

15 All day long my disgrace is before me, and shame has covered my face

16 at the sound of the taunter and reviler, at the sight of the enemy and the avenger.

17 All this has come upon us, though we have not forgotten you, and we have not been false to your covenant.

18 Our heart has not turned back, nor have our steps departed from your way;

19 yet you have broken us in the place of jackals and covered us with the shadow of death.

20 If we had forgotten the name of our God or spread out our hands to a foreign god,

21 would not God discover this? For he knows the secrets of the heart.

22 Yet for your sake we are killed all the day long; we are regarded as sheep to be slaughtered.

23 Awake! Why are you sleeping, O Lord? Rouse yourself! Do not reject us forever!

24 Why do you hide your face? Why do you forget our affliction and oppression?

25 For our soul is bowed down to the dust; our belly clings to the ground.

26 Rise up; come to our help! Redeem us for the sake of your steadfast love!

neighbors, even as we care for them. We hear the derision and scorn of those around us. They proclaim that we are intolerant, even while we love them. You have made Your people a laughingstock among the citizens in our own community.

As trials come upon us, we do not forget You. Some of us remain faithful to Your Word. You break us in the ruins of our nation. You cover us with the shadow of death.

If a time of trial and testing must come, then let it be from Your hand for the purposes of Your will. Do not let it be judgment brought on because we forgot You. Protect us from worshipping counterfeit gods. If we must die every day because we stand boldly in Your Name, let us first put to death our pride and our selfish desires so that we may stand without flinching. Let those who watch the way we die know with certainty that You are our King, oh God.

Psalm 45

1. My heart overflows with a pleasing theme; I address my verses to the king; my tongue is like the pen of a ready scribe.

2. You are the most handsome of the sons of men; grace is poured upon your lips; therefore God has blessed you forever.

3. Gird your sword on your thigh, O mighty one, in your splendor and majesty!

4. In your majesty ride out victoriously for the cause of truth and meekness and righteousness; let your right hand teach you awesome deeds!

5. Your arrows are sharp in the heart of the king's enemies; the peoples fall under you.

6. Your throne, O God, is forever and ever. The scepter of your kingdom is a scepter of uprightness;

7. you have loved righteousness and hated wickedness. Therefore God, your God, has anointed you with the oil of gladness beyond your companions;

8. your robes are all fragrant with myrrh and aloes and cassia. From ivory palaces stringed instruments make you glad;

9. daughters of kings are among your ladies of honor; at your right hand stands the queen in gold of Ophir.

10. Hear, O daughter, and consider, and incline your ear: forget your people and your father's house,

11. and the king will desire your beauty. Since he is your lord, bow to him.

12. The people of Tyre will seek your favor with gifts, the richest of the people.

The Marriage Celebration

Father, I love this psalm. I see in it the most splendid description of the marriage supper of Jesus Christ for His pure and holy bride, the church. Let me always be ready and able to proclaim the beauty of this marvelous event.

Is there a man more handsome than the Son of Man? Jesus, when You came to earth as the Suffering Servant, You had no beauty to draw us to You. After the abuse leading to Your crucifixion, You looked hardly human. As the resurrected King of glory, your beauty is majestic. Grace and mercy pour from your lips as You intercede for us at the right hand of the Father. All power to fulfill the purpose of the Father belongs to You.

The day will soon come when You return to the earth. In Your majesty, You will ride out victoriously, destroying Your enemies, subduing the nations. This is the vision of the reigning, Royal Bridegroom.

Yet another day comes, oh God, that fills the heart of the Bridegroom with great joy. Before Your throne in heaven You will anoint Your only begotten Son with the oil of incomparable gladness. His robes will be fragrant with the spices of incense. Songs of celebration will sound from the heavenly palaces. His royal attendants will be the daughters of kings. At Your Son's side will be his bride, the queen He came to earth to claim. She will be dressed in garments of glorious colors and purest gold.

Even now from Your lips, Sovereign Father, comes Your command to the church, the Bride of Christ: "Listen to Me, My daughter. Your loyalty and faith belong to My Son. He desires and loves you above all creation. Submit to Him and be blessed. People of great wealth will pour out their riches to find favor with you."

You say to us as we wait for that day, "You are the glorious church on earth, the princess preparing in her chamber for the summons of the King. On the day prepared, you will be called to enter—with joy and gladness—into the presence of your Lord."

You, Sovereign God, will bless this marriage with righteousness and eternal praise.

While we wait for the Bridegroom to come for His bride, bless every marriage between a godly man and a godly woman. Let their marriage show us a picture of this royal union to come so that we yearn for that day.

13 All glorious is the princess in her chamber, with robes interwoven with gold.

14 In many-colored robes she is led to the king, with her virgin companions following behind her.

15 With joy and gladness they are led along as they enter the palace of the king.

16 In place of your fathers shall be your sons; you will make them princes in all the earth.

17 I will cause your name to be remembered in all generations; therefore nations will praise you forever and ever.

My Prayer

Psalm 46

1 God is our refuge and strength, a very present help in trouble.

2 Therefore we will not fear though the earth gives way, though the mountains be moved into the heart of the sea,

3 though its waters roar and foam, though the mountains tremble at its swelling.

Selah

4 There is a river whose streams make glad the city of God, the holy habitation of the Most High.

5 God is in the midst of her; she shall not be moved; God will help her when morning dawns.

6 The nations rage, the kingdoms totter; he utters his voice, the earth melts.

7 The Lord of hosts is with us; the God of Jacob is our fortress.

Selah

8 Come, behold the works of the Lord, how he has brought desolations on the earth.

9 He makes wars cease to the end of the earth; he breaks the bow and shatters the spear; he burns the chariots with fire.

10 "Be still, and know that I am God. I will be exalted among the nations, I will be exalted in the earth!"

11 The Lord of hosts is with us; the God of Jacob is our fortress.

City of Safety

Oh Lord God of the universe, the technology of our society forms such a fragile structure. We take the elements of the world You created—air, fire, water, and earth—and turn them into spider webs, then consider ourselves lords of the universe. How proud we are of our tinsel towns.

Suddenly, You shudder the ground with an earthquake or roil the oceans with a tsunami and then crumple our structures like cardboard toys. Hurricanes, tornadoes, blizzards, flash floods, and mudslides teach us that we control only the thinnest margins of Your world. The portion we control is only by Your permission and with the continuous grace that You pour out upon us.

Every nation, every city, every person is proud of our haughty towers. What pain and suffering we experience when, by the "natural events" in the world, You remove them from our grasp. In a moment, You sweep away lives and property. Survivors look around for someone to blame.

Our lack of control is even more obvious with disasters created by man. When humanity makes war upon itself, we do so only because You have removed Your restraints. Every day You hold back our inbred hatred and greed. Should You not restrain us, we would never know even temporary peace. Yet time and again, war explodes. As with other crises, You desire that this trouble drive us to our knees, confessing that our lives are in Your hands.

Nevertheless, we fail to humble ourselves and cry out to You. Instead, we turn our pride into anger and bitterness. We raise our fists and shake them at You for thwarting us. Should we not praise You as Job did? He lost everyone and everything except his wife and his life and still said, "The Lord gives and the Lord takes away. Blessed be the Name of the Lord."

Each time You prove to us the futility of our selfish grasp, You show us that You are our only refuge and strength. We can find redemption only in You. Yet though we rail against You, You love us enough to wait until we humble ourselves and confess that our lives are in Your hands.

The time is coming, Lord of hosts, when through natural and man-made disasters, You bring desolation on the earth. Every day until then, continue to draw us to You. Continue to burn away our pride. Bring us into Your kingdom. Place us in the City of Safety where none can destroy. Be, oh God of Jacob, our fortress.

Psalm 47

1. Clap your hands, all peoples! Shout to God with loud songs of joy!

2. For the Lord, the Most High, is to be feared, a great king over all the earth.

3. He subdued peoples under us, and nations under our feet.

4. He chose our heritage for us, the pride of Jacob whom he loves.

    Selah

5. God has gone up with a shout, the Lord with the sound of a trumpet.

6. Sing praises to God, sing praises! Sing praises to our King, sing praises!

7. For God is the King of all the earth; sing praises with a psalm!

8. God reigns over the nations; God sits on his holy throne.

9. The princes of the peoples gather as the people of the God of Abraham. For the shields of the earth belong to God; he is highly exalted!

A Greater Gathering

All over the world, oh God—at this exact moment—some of Your children praise You in their hearts and with their lips. Our worship brings glory to You and joy to us. How much more is Your glory and our joy magnified when we gather in one place to praise You with our music and worship You with our prayers?

We sing, "Great is our God!" We give You a standing ovation, confessing with the sound of our clapping hands that You are the Lord Most High, worthy of worship. We proclaim in our prayers, "You are the King over all the nations."

Oh, great God, You chose us to share in the heritage of Jacob. Through Jesus, Your firstborn son, You prepare for us a greater gathering in which we will worship You with the most intense joy.

On that great and terrible day, Your children will answer Your mighty trumpet blast with a wildly enthusiastically joyful shout. Our thunderous song of praise will vibrate the air, ripple the seas, and rock the earth. You will be revealed to enemies and friends alike as King over all the earth. Every living being will bow either in fear or in reverence as You take Your seat on Your holy throne. As You sit on Your throne and reign over the nations, Your children will gather before You, proclaiming in a united choir too large to number, "You, oh God, are highly exalted! The congregation of the righteous shall praise you forever."

Psalm 48

1. Great is the Lord and greatly to be praised in the city of our God! His holy mountain,

2. O beautiful in elevation, is the joy of all the earth, Mount Zion, in the far north, the city of the great King.

3. Within her citadels God has made himself known as a fortress.

4. For behold, the kings assembled; they came on together.

5. As soon as they saw it, they were astounded; they were in panic; they took to flight.

6. Trembling took hold of them there, anguish as of a woman in labor.

7. By the east wind you shattered the ships of Tarshish.

8. As we have heard, so have we seen in the city of the Lord of hosts, in the city of our God, which God will establish forever.

   Selah

9. We have thought on your steadfast love, O God, in the midst of your temple.

10. As your name, O God, so your praise reaches to the ends of the earth. Your right hand is filled with righteousness.

11. Let Mount Zion be glad! Let the daughters of Judah rejoice because of your judgments!

12. Walk about Zion, go around her, number her towers,

13. consider well her ramparts, go through her citadels, that you may tell the next generation

14. that this is God, our God forever and ever. He will guide us forever.

Jerusalem, City of Supernatural Peace

Holy, holy, holy are You, oh Lord God Almighty! The earth is only Your footstool, yet You chose to greatly bless one city. You named it The City of God, The City of Peace—Jerusalem.

Your temple, built on the elevation of Mount Zion, saw centuries of praise festivals and humble worship from Your children. Even though—time after time—enemies destroyed Your temple, You always sent Your servants to restore it. I praise You, God, for the day of worship in Your temple will come again.

No matter how many times Your enemies thought that they had destroyed Your city, regardless of the number of shrines to false gods and idols they dedicated on the site of Your temple, they have always failed. We will not be dismayed over our enemies' apparent victories. Instead, we remember that You are Jerusalem's protection, her stronghold, her fortress.

How often have the kings assembled against Jerusalem? In recent days, You recreated Israel by the stroke of a pen in the hands of the United Nations. From that day in 1947 to this one, You have continuously protected Jerusalem from destruction. Thank you, merciful God.

You astound the nations as You display your care for Your chosen people. You engage the relentless march of Your purpose to reign over all the earth from Your throne on Mount Zion.

You established Jerusalem as the eternal capital city.

Jesus died and was raised from the dead in Jerusalem. In the future, He will reign from there as King of kings and Lord of hosts. We will praise Your Name so that it reaches the ends of the earth as You judge the nations according to their treatment of Jerusalem. We will rejoice because Your judgment is righteous.

Today, we move about Jerusalem, walking her streets, touching the walls, viewing the towers. On streets laid over thousands of years of history, a vibrant city pulses with life, hope, fear, and war. The one thing missing from the city is peace.

As You have charged us, I pray, today, for the peace of Jerusalem. I ask not for the peace that comes with death and destruction of those

My Prayer

who wage war against the Israelis. I ask for hostilities between Israel and her neighbors to cease, but not only that. I plead for a greater peace. I cry for Your loving peace to descend on all of the Middle East. Let such an anointing of the Holy Spirit fall on both Jews and non-Jews that the greatest outpouring of salvation in all of history ignites. Begin it, please, in Jerusalem. Then, regardless of events in the nations, Jerusalem and her neighbors will have peace with You—the ultimate eternal peace.

Psalm 49

1 Hear this, all peoples! Give ear, all inhabitants of the world,

2 both low and high, rich and poor together!

3 My mouth shall speak wisdom; the meditation of my heart shall be understanding.

4 I will incline my ear to a proverb; I will solve my riddle to the music of the lyre.

5 Why should I fear in times of trouble, when the iniquity of those who cheat me surrounds me,

6 those who trust in their wealth and boast of the abundance of their riches?

7 Truly no man can ransom another, or give to God the price of his life,

8 for the ransom of their life is costly and can never suffice,

9 that he should live on forever and never see the pit.

10 For he sees that even the wise die; the fool and the stupid alike must perish and leave their wealth to others.

11 Their graves are their homes forever, their dwelling places to all generations, though they called lands by their own names.

12 Man in his pomp will not remain; he is like the beasts that perish.

13 This is the path of those who have foolish confidence; yet after them people approve of their boasts.

Selah

DEATH SHALL BE THEIR SHEPHERD

Look at all the people, Lord—six billion and growing. Across the world, every country has rich and poor, high and low, ordinary citizens and wicked people. Yes, in every country, You have faithful followers. (Thank You for Your grace poured out upon us.)

As I read about people in different countries, I find a puzzling fact: many who are blessed with wealth engage in criminal acts. Why, Lord? Most people earn money by working hard and using their talents wisely. Yet some people devote their lives to stealing from others to gain great wealth. What does that wealth buy them? They may gain followers who applaud their every action, gain access to seats of power, and gain elegant estates, but it cannot buy them life.

Trouble comes to all people—war, disease, and at the end of this life, death. Can those with wealth do more than carve their names on buildings or put their names on pieces of land? No, they perish and leave their wealth to others.

In the end, their fate will be the same as all the others who trust in themselves: death will be their shepherd. Death will come for them, pulling them with the crook on the end of its staff to destruction. Death will not gently gather them to its chest for comfort. It will give them what they always thought they wanted—eternal separation from God. It will deliver what they always feared the most—eternal punishment and pain.

Before it is too late, oh Lord, call them to Yourself with songs of love. Show them the futility of trusting in themselves and in the wealth of this world to save them. Show them the hollow decay at the center of their lives. Envelop them in Your grace and mercy. Wash them in the blood You shed for their sins. Vanquish death. Give them life. Be their Shepherd.

14 Like sheep they are appointed for Sheol; Death shall be their shepherd, and the upright shall rule over them in the morning. Their form shall be consumed in Sheol, with no place to dwell.

15 But God will ransom my soul from the power of Sheol, for he will receive me.

Selah

16 Be not afraid when a man becomes rich, when the glory of his house increases.

17 For when he dies he will carry nothing away; his glory will not go down after him.

18 For though, while he lives, he counts himself blessed—and though you get praise when you do well for yourself—

19 his soul will go to the generation of his fathers, who will never again see light.

20 Man in his pomp yet without understanding is like the beasts that perish.

My Prayer

Psalm 50

1. The Mighty One, God the Lord, speaks and summons the earth from the rising of the sun to its setting.

2. Out of Zion, the perfection of beauty, God shines forth.

3. Our God comes; he does not keep silence; before him is a devouring fire, around him a mighty tempest.

4. He calls to the heavens above and to the earth, that he may judge his people:

5. "Gather to me my faithful ones, who made a covenant with me by sacrifice!"

6. The heavens declare his righteousness, for God himself is judge!

   Selah

7. "Hear, O my people, and I will speak; O Israel, I will testify against you. I am God, your God.

8. Not for your sacrifices do I rebuke you; your burnt offerings are continually before me.

9. I will not accept a bull from your house or goats from your folds.

10. For every beast of the forest is mine, the cattle on a thousand hills.

11. I know all the birds of the hills, and all that moves in the field is mine.

12. "If I were hungry, I would not tell you, for the world and its fullness are mine.

13. Do I eat the flesh of bulls or drink the blood of goats?

14. Offer to God a sacrifice of thanksgiving, and perform your vows to the Most High,

Thankful Hearts

You, oh Mighty One, are not surprised by the confusion, false teaching, and hypocrisy found in churches around the world. You give each congregation a purpose and a role to play in Your kingdom, knowing all the while that not every person who calls himself a Christian is Your child. From the rising of the sun to its setting, in each congregation, You display Your righteous rule just as You did from the Temple on Mount Zion, centuries ago.

As God of Your people, You rightly speak to us who claim to be part of Your kingdom. Open our ears and our hearts to hear what You tell us:

"For you who are cleansed by the blood of the Lamb, stop showing off. Yes, you attend church regularly, you give your money to support the work of the church, you even give your free time to church activities. However, you also make sure that everyone knows about it.

"Do I need you to do these things? No! I own the wealth of the whole world and everyone in it. I have no need that you can fill.

"I created you to be a member of My family. Attend church, give your money, give your time, and obey Me because your heart overflows with thanksgiving. When your humble thanksgiving takes center stage, your pride evaporates. When you are without pride, you gladly turn to Me. When you depend on Me, the windows of heaven open and I deliver you. Your thanksgiving, your obedience, and your dependence display My glory.

"For everyone else who comes to My church, I ask this question: What gives you the right to call yourself a Christian? You refuse to repent of your sins and be washed in the blood of My Son. Instead, you ignore My Words in the Bible and resent the discipline that I bring into your life. When you talk to sinners who are searching for the way to Me, you tell them, "Don't worry, God will accept you just the way you are. You don't need to do anything." Cursing comes from your heart and mouth. Your own family fears you. Yet, because I am patient with you, you feel contempt for Me.

"Pay attention! Repent of your evil ways; call on Me for forgiveness of your sins. If you don't, I will tear your life apart and no one will deliver you from My hand.

"Those who seek My Son with all their hearts find My salvation. Those who live their lives from thankful hearts display My glory. Well done."

15 and call upon me in the day of trouble; I will deliver you, and you shall glorify me."

16 But to the wicked God says: "What right have you to recite my statutes or take my covenant on your lips?

17 For you hate discipline, and you cast my words behind you.

18 If you see a thief, you are pleased with him, and you keep company with adulterers.

19 "You give your mouth free rein for evil, and your tongue frames deceit.

20 You sit and speak against your brother; you slander your own mother's son.

21 These things you have done, and I have been silent; you thought that I was one like yourself. But now I rebuke you and lay the charge before you.

22 "Mark this, then, you who forget God, lest I tear you apart, and there be none to deliver!

23 The one who offers thanksgiving as his sacrifice glorifies me; to one who orders his way rightly I will show the salvation of God!"

My Prayer

Psalm 51

1. Have mercy on me, O God, according to your steadfast love; according to your abundant mercy blot out my transgressions.

2. Wash me thoroughly from my iniquity, and cleanse me from my sin!

3. For I know my transgressions, and my sin is ever before me.

4. Against you, you only, have I sinned and done what is evil in your sight, so that you may be justified in your words and blameless in your judgment.

5. Behold, I was brought forth in iniquity, and in sin did my mother conceive me.

6. Behold, you delight in truth in the inward being, and you teach me wisdom in the secret heart.

7. Purge me with hyssop, and I shall be clean; wash me, and I shall be whiter than snow.

8. Let me hear joy and gladness; let the bones that you have broken rejoice.

9. Hide your face from my sins, and blot out all my iniquities.

10. Create in me a clean heart, O God, and renew a right spirit within me.

11. Cast me not away from your presence, and take not your Holy Spirit from me.

12. Restore to me the joy of your salvation, and uphold me with a willing spirit.

13. Then I will teach transgressors your ways, and sinners will return to you.

Restore to Me the Treasures of Heaven

Father, I come crying for Your mercy. I confess. I did the unthinkable; I publically dishonored Your Name.

Even as I sinned, I excused my actions. I told myself, "I deserve to relax and let off steam. I'm not really hurting anybody. No one will ever find out." How could I believe my own lies so easily?

Now, everyone knows. Every day I see the shock and disbelief in the eyes of my family. Faithful friends, who loyally stood beside me when the rumors started, are brokenhearted. Most of them avoid me because of the pain of my betrayal. People whisper to each other and laugh behind my back as I walk down the street.

I knew when I did it that it was wrong. I thought I could get away with it. How had I drifted so far that I could ignore You? My sin—that hurt so many people—was rebellion against You. You see everything. You saw me throw open the door to evil. You watched me betray You.

You could have easily left me in my sin. Instead, You took what I did in secret and confronted me with it in public. Your words were true when mine were lies. Your verdict was just, Your judgment righteous.

The things I did because I love You—attend church, study my Bible, sing songs of worship, spend time with You in prayer—became first an empty routine, then a hypocritical act. Where we once shared joy and gladness, I had a hollow facade. Those activities that, like bones, supported and nourished our relationship, were crushed.

Father, I am your runaway child come home. You never let go of me as I walked away from You. You had washed me in the blood of Your Son. You had blotted from The Book of Judgment all my sins. Those facts remained even in the face of my rebellion.

Yet my loss was almost as great as if I had lost my salvation. I lost Your companionship. I lost the sweet whisper of the Holy Spirit guiding me in all my ways. I lost the inexpressible joy of serving You. How could I throw away the treasures of heaven for the filth of this world?

I collapse in shame before You. Have mercy on me according to Your steadfast love.

14 Deliver me from bloodguiltiness, O God, O God of my salvation, and my tongue will sing aloud of your righteousness.

15 O Lord, open my lips, and my mouth will declare your praise.

16 For you will not delight in sacrifice, or I would give it; you will not be pleased with a burnt offering.

17 The sacrifices of God are a broken spirit; a broken and contrite heart, O God, you will not despise.

18 Do good to Zion in your good pleasure; build up the walls of Jerusalem;

19 then will you delight in right sacrifices, in burnt offerings and whole burnt offerings; then bulls will be offered on your altar.

When I accepted the gift of salvation by faith in Jesus, You took my heart of stone and replaced it with a heart of flesh. I soiled that new heart and stained it with evil. Please cleanse my heart. Replace the darkness of sin. Remove the glare of guilt from my vision and restore the ability to see You, and the power to hear You. Restore to me the joy of my salvation.

I have shamed Your Name, but by Your grace, that will not be the end. As You restore and uphold me, I will sing aloud of Your righteousness. I will publically confess my sin. I will confess my failure to uphold the holiness of Your Name. I will be accountable as Your servants test my restoration. I will again rejoice in the power of Your Word to give life, hear the whisper of the Holy Spirit, and know the joy of serving You. I will display Your glory as You restore to me the treasures of heaven.

Psalm 52

1. Why do you boast of evil, O mighty man? The steadfast love of God endures all the day.

2. Your tongue plots destruction, like a sharp razor, you worker of deceit.

3. You love evil more than good, and lying more than speaking what is right.

   Selah

4. You love all words that devour, O deceitful tongue.

5. But God will break you down forever; he will snatch and tear you from your tent; he will uproot you from the land of the living.

   Selah

6. The righteous shall see and fear, and shall laugh at him, saying,

7. "See the man who would not make God his refuge, but trusted in the abundance of his riches and sought refuge in his own destruction!"

8. But I am like a green olive tree in the house of God. I trust in the steadfast love of God forever and ever.

9. I will thank you forever, because you have done it. I will wait for your name, for it is good, in the presence of the godly.

The Wealth of Sand Castles

Lord God, I come to You with a burning desire for vengeance engulfing my mind. Yet, You claim vengeance as Your right.

I understand that You love me always and protect me every day. However certain events drained away much of my life. It's not fair! Allow me at least to lay all my ugly feelings before You.

There is a man with a high position in our community who gathers rumors and entices gossip, then weaves a blanket of lies. He plans a campaign to destroy his target and to devour his victim. He gains his position by climbing the backs of those he brings down. He takes extra delight when he threatens one of Your children. Now he attacks me!

Who am I that he desires my destruction? My small business does not threaten his. I have no power or high standing in our community. I have only my reputation as a fair and honest person who loves You. Everyone who meets me learns about my passion to display Your glory.

Can his plan to smother me in lies succeed? What will he gain by destroying my business? He may even succeed in destroying my reputation, but he will *never* take away Your love!

You are the Holy, Righteous God and Your vengeance is an unstoppable tide. This man wallows in his own destruction, as he trusts in the power and wealth his vicious lifestyle has erected. To You his power is like the power of seaweed and his wealth like the wealth of sand castles. When death calls, nothing in his life will help him. Then, at The Judgment, those who suffered from his evil tongue will stand as witnesses against him. As one who never sought forgiveness from You, he has no defense.

So here I am: angry, frustrated, and hungry for vengeance. Nevertheless, I release this man and this situation to You. If You use him to separate me from my business and my work, then I am ready to move in a new direction. You're the Boss.

Regardless of the outcome, I trust in Your steadfast love. Even if he destroys my reputation and I am shunned, You will make me as fruitful as an olive tree. You will continue to pour out Your love through me and to display Your glory in my life. I will focus my life on You and let You take care of him.

Psalm 53

1. The fool says in his heart, "There is no God." They are corrupt, doing abominable iniquity; there is none who does good.

2. God looks down from heaven on the children of man to see if there are any who understand, who seek after God.

3. They have all fallen away; together they have become corrupt; there is none who does good, not even one.

4. Have those who work evil no knowledge, who eat up my people as they eat bread, and do not call upon God?

5. There they are, in great terror, where there is no terror! For God scatters the bones of him who encamps against you; you put them to shame, for God has rejected them.

6. Oh, that salvation for Israel would come out of Zion! When God restores the fortunes of his people, let Jacob rejoice, let Israel be glad.

Fools and Followers

Father God from whom no one hides, how can You be so patient with humanity? You see the hearts of all people. You compare each thought and every action against Your holiness. Not one person meets Your standard. We are born seeking our own way. We grow in ignorance and mature in committing corrupt, abominable acts. In the depths of our depravity we become fools who loudly proclaim, "God does not exist!"

And yet and yet, You—in Your boundless love and in Your great mercy—snatch some of us out of our depravity. You open our eyes to our need of forgiveness. You give us faith to believe in the Name of Jesus. You adopt us into Your family. By Your omnipotence, You call out fools and turn them into sons. You divide humanity into fools and followers.

Fools feel idiotic hating a nonexistent god, but they eagerly hate Your followers. They might hide behind some form of religion, but the more they embrace evil in their hearts and display it in their actions, the more they persecute Your people. In every community of every nation, fools seek victory over those who follow You. *They strike us down, but they cannot destroy us!*

The knowledge that Your people cannot be destroyed brings terror to every fool's heart. Behind the mask of scorn hides a person who sees death summoning him. He also sees Your followers viewing the same summons without fear. (Fools cannot see that Your followers walk in the valley of the shadow of death with You by their side.)

Thank You, Father, for allowing those who rebel against You to feel fear. By that fear, some will recognize their danger. They will repent and follow You.

For those who refuse to acknowledge You, that terror is not an empty threat. They die and their bones are scattered. Their arrogant declaration of rejection—"There is no god"—now shames them as You eternally reject them. They watch Your followers rejoice with great gladness as You restore their fortunes.

In the agony of their eviction from Your presence, they recognize—in agony and with great bitterness—that they are fools forever.

Psalm 54

1. God, save me, by your name, and vindicate me by your might.
2. O God, hear my prayer; give ear to the words of my mouth.
3. For strangers have risen against me; ruthless men seek my life; they do not set God before themselves.

    Selah

4. Behold, God is my helper; the Lord is the upholder of my life.
5. He will return the evil to my enemies; in your faithfulness put an end to them.
6. With a freewill offering I will sacrifice to you; I will give thanks to your name, O Lord, for it is good.
7. For he has delivered me from every trouble, and my eye has looked in triumph on my enemies.

The Vindicator

Hear my prayer, oh God. I turn to You in my distress. My great distress erupts from an angry heart. How many Christians must lose their lives because of their faith in You? How many children must become orphans because their parents remained faithful to You? Vindicate them by your might, Almighty One.

Unlike Your martyrs, I live in an oasis of peace. Yet even in this place of quiet, men who have no regard for Your holiness attack me. They attack my spiritual life instead of my body. They subtly draw me away from You through the movies I attend, the TV shows I watch, the news reports I hear, and the books I read. I feel like Lot living in Sodom; the wanton ways of the ungodly and lawless torment me.

As hard as I fight against it, I absorb some of the lies they speak. My heart becomes callous to the unspeakable evil that my culture considers acceptable behavior. Even when I am wary, some of their plots ambush me. When I faint with weariness, their ambushes sometimes trap me. Lord, unless You sustain me, I will not escape their brainwashing. Without You constantly shielding and sustaining me in this battle, I cannot stand.

Father, let evil recoil on those whose agenda is to pull down the children in Your kingdom. Destroy the effectiveness of those who are tools of the devil. The devil wants to slander me before You. Vindicate me by Your might.

Thank You, Lord, for giving me victory in this battle. Even now, a grand party celebrating our victory rocks heaven with praise to You. Those who were martyred for their faith already celebrate in triumph. When You have delivered me from all my troubles, I will join them in heaven, praising You, the One Who Vindicates.

Psalm 55:1–16

1. Give ear to my prayer, O God, and hide not yourself from my plea for mercy!

2. Attend to me, and answer me; I am restless in my complaint and I moan,

3. because of the noise of the enemy, because of the oppression of the wicked. For they drop trouble upon me, and in anger they bear a grudge against me.

4. My heart is in anguish within me; the terrors of death have fallen upon me.

5. Fear and trembling come upon me, and horror overwhelms me.

6. And I say, "Oh, that I had wings like a dove! I would fly away and be at rest;

7. yes, I would wander far away; I would lodge in the wilderness;

   Selah

8. I would hurry to find a shelter from the raging wind and tempest."

9. Destroy, O Lord, divide their tongues; for I see violence and strife in the city.

10. Day and night they go around it on its walls, and iniquity and trouble are within it;

11. ruin is in its midst; oppression and fraud do not depart from its marketplace.

12. For it is not an enemy who taunts me—then I could bear it; it is not an adversary who deals insolently with me—then I could hide from him.

Betrayed!

God, help! My heart pounds; I gasp for air. Hear me, Lord. I'm desperate for You. Answer me, my God, for I despair of life.

I try to hold everything together, to focus my mind, when other people are present. That's all an act. Even then, I am panic-stricken. Alone, my whole body shakes. Coffee splashes over my fingers. Makeup turns me into a clown face.

When will this stop? My husband abandoned me. Now every day he brings a new demand. Every night he delivers a new threat. He's never satisfied. He torments me. I think he will be satisfied only with my destruction.

God, how could this happen? My mind and my emotions are battered. Horror blankets my mind. Terror so devastating that it seems to be a visit from death saturates my emotions. Help, Lord!

You know what I really want to do, God? I want to run away. If I could just go some place safe and cry for a week … I need to fly away to a place where no one knows me. If only I could disappear for a while so I could think and talk to You. Shelter me, Lord, for I don't know how I can go through this.

It was bad enough when he was the only one harassing me. Now he's hired a lawyer. Day and night they talk over their strategies. Confuse them, Lord. Instead of clear communications, cause them to misunderstand each other. Lead them to misinterpret the law. Reward their malice and mischief toward me with violence and ruin.

Lord, I still don't believe this is happening. It has to be a nightmare. I'll wake up with my husband's warm body nestled close to mine, snugly secure in his arms.

How could he betray me like this? After twenty years, how could he reject me by announcing on my birthday that he wanted a divorce? My lover, my companion, my best friend walked out!

Where is the man I married? The one I thought I knew inside and out? I thought we shared our hearts with each other. We worshipped You together and served in our church. When did this evil enter our marriage? How did he get so far away from You?

Lord, I thought that we shared a rich and loving relationship centered on You. I lost that; it was snatched away. Yet I have not lost You. I call on You to save me, for I cannot save myself.

13 But it is you, a man, my equal, my companion, my familiar friend.

14 We used to take sweet counsel together; within God's house we walked in the throng.

15 Let death steal over them; let them go down to Sheol alive; for evil is in their dwelling place and in their heart.

16 But I call to God, and the Lord will save me.

My Prayer

Psalm 55:17–23

17 Evening and morning and at noon I utter my complaint and moan, and he hears my voice.

18 He redeems my soul in safety from the battle that I wage, for many are arrayed against me.

19 God will give ear and humble them, he who is enthroned from of old,

Selah

because they do not change and do not fear God.

20 My companion stretched out his hand against his friends; he violated his covenant.

21 His speech was smooth as butter, yet war was in his heart; his words were softer than oil, yet they were drawn swords.

22 Cast your burden on the Lord, and he will sustain you; he will never permit the righteous to be moved.

23 But you, O God, will cast them down into the pit of destruction; men of blood and treachery shall not live out half their days. But I will trust in you.

Shattered on a Sure Foundation

I wish I could tell You the depths of my loneliness, Lord. I think constantly about my wife's betrayal. My head hurts, my stomach aches, and all I want to do is sleep. Yet when I lie down, I can't stop thinking about this mess and actually sleep! Instead, I see memory movies.

We had our perfect wedding at church. We spoke our vows before You; family and friends witnessed them. She's broken that promise. Was her heart not in it? Through years of happiness and times of trial, we gave each other love and comfort. Now those memories cut me into a thousand pieces.

What did I miss? How could I have been so blind? How did I fail? I loved this woman and was devoted to her. Now I continually question my ability to see what is real and true.

Not satisfied with breaking my heart and destroying our marriage, my wife wants to take away my children. She wants to take all I have, leaving me with nothing. She wants to destroy my life.

Oh God, what can I do? This burden is too great for me to carry. I see only my wife's treachery and the tragedy of our divorce. Even so, You are my sure foundation. Nothing she does will move me from this place. Nevertheless, Lord, I lie shattered here. Collect my splintered pieces and put me back together again. Strengthen my faith and increase my ability to understand people. Take my loneliness. Replace it with joy in Your fellowship.

As my wife runs toward an empty life, give her barrenness. When she reaches bottom, remind her of Your love. It won't un-break my heart, but it could heal hers. All I can do is shelter in Your love. Carry me through this flood of bitter pain and this fire of divorce. Restore my shattered heart.

Psalm 56

1. Be gracious to me, O God, for man tramples on me; all day long an attacker oppresses me;

2. my enemies trample on me all day long, for many attack me proudly.

3. When I am afraid, I put my trust in you.

4. In God, whose word I praise, in God I trust; I shall not be afraid. What can flesh do to me?

5. All day long they injure my cause; all their thoughts are against me for evil.

6. They stir up strife, they lurk; they watch my steps, as they have waited for my life.

7. For their crime will they escape? In wrath cast down the peoples, O God!

8. You have kept count of my tossings; put my tears in your bottle. Are they not in your book?

9. Then my enemies will turn back in the day when I call. This I know, that God is for me.

10. In God, whose word I praise, in the Lord, whose word I praise,

11. in God I trust; I shall not be afraid. What can man do to me?

12. I must perform my vows to you, O God; I will render thank offerings to you.

13. For you have delivered my soul from death, yes, my feet from falling, that I may walk before God in the light of life.

I Choose to Live in Praise

Father, I think my mind is playing tricks on me. For the third time, I felt as though someone was following me as I walked home. How weird when I never see anyone even looking in my direction. Yet I am uneasy and relax only when I stand behind my locked door.

Do I imagine someone stalking me? How can I know? Should I call the police? Tell a friend? I have no proof. The only thing certain is that I am afraid.

Shall I let this fear take over my life? Will I let the *possibility* of someone spying on my movements control the way I think and feel? No! When I am afraid, I will trust in You.

Even if I listen to my intuition and become more careful about when and where I go, I refuse to let fear control of my life. A person may shadow me, but You are always my companion. You give Your angels charge over me, to guide me in all my ways.

You are greater than anyone or anything that threatens me. I chose to trust you and to live with courage, facing my fear in the strength You give me.

I choose to live in praise of You, not in fear of anyone. Because You gave me new life in Christ, I have eternal life. Can mere human power steal this life? No! Someone might separate my body from my soul. If so, my soul, like a helium balloon released in the air, would ascend to Your throne in heaven. I choose to trust in You and find joy in my days. I choose to praise Your Name.

Psalm 57

1. Be merciful to me, O God, be merciful to me, for in you my soul takes refuge; in the shadow of your wings I will take refuge, till the storms of destruction pass by.

2. I cry out to God Most High, to God who fulfills his purpose for me.

3. He will send from heaven and save me; he will put to shame him who tramples on me.

   Selah

   God will send out his steadfast love and his faithfulness!

4. My soul is in the midst of lions; I lie down amid fiery beasts—the children of man, whose teeth are spears and arrows, whose tongues are sharp swords.

5. Be exalted, O God, above the heavens! Let your glory be over all the earth!

6. They set a net for my steps; my soul was bowed down. They dug a pit in my way, but they have fallen into it themselves.

   Selah

7. My heart is steadfast, O God, my heart is steadfast! I will sing and make melody!

8. Awake, my glory! Awake, O harp and lyre! I will awake the dawn!

9. I will give thanks to you, O Lord, among the peoples; I will sing praises to you among the nations.

10. For your steadfast love is great to the heavens, your faithfulness to the clouds.

11. Be exalted, O God, above the heavens! Let your glory be over all the earth!

Storms Cannot Destroy

Father, who am I that You give me refuge? Most people huddle together with their backs to the storm, without a refuge. Yet in Your great mercy, You drew me close to You. Like a mother bird with her baby chick, You spread Your wings over me, covering me with Your feathers.

Great storms of destruction straddle the earth. Like an overactive hurricane season, one storm follows on the heels of another. Stress mounts like a flood as ruin multiplies.

I stay alert, preparing for another storm even as I work on the recovery effort from the previous one. Rather than wait for the dark clouds of destruction to loom on the horizon before I seek refuge, I keep close to Your side every day.

Your mercies are new every morning. Daily You send out Your steadfast love. No one can divert me from fulfilling Your purpose for my life. When Satan tries to trample me, You transform his evil intentions into glorious blessings. You shame him by showing the world that he is powerless.

Even when the destructive storm is caused by man, I lie down and sleep in peace. Men, whose every thought and word are weapons of destruction, cannot reach me in my refuge. They may surround me, but You shield me.

Let those who huddle together trying to shelter from the storm see that I stand on unshaken ground in the shadow of the Almighty. Show storm-tossed people that You are powerful above all the storms and that You are forever faithful.

What does it matter if traps lay in my path? Like a blind person who walks on the edge of a cliff yet never falls, I trust You to guide me according to Your plan. Even in the danger of the storm and on the edge of the cliff, my heart sings. My mouth makes a melody in praise of You. I cannot contain my joy as I experience Your steadfast love and faithfulness through another storm's passing.

I awake with the dawn singing of Your great mercies. I rush to tell my friends about Your protection. I plead with everyone to seek refuge in You. Gladly, I recount Your steadfast love. Joyfully, I display Your faithfulness.

I shall not rest until everyone knows of the eternal refuge that can only be found in You. Cover the earth in Your glory until all are safely shielded from the storms.

Psalm 58

1 Do you indeed decree what is right, you gods? Do you judge the children of man uprightly?

2 No, in your hearts you devise wrongs; your hands deal out violence on earth.

3 The wicked are estranged from the womb; they go astray from birth, speaking lies.

4 They have venom like the venom of a serpent, like the deaf adder that stops its ear,

5 so that it does not hear the voice of charmers or of the cunning enchanter.

6 O God, break the teeth in their mouths; tear out the fangs of the young lions, O Lord!

7 Let them vanish like water that runs away; when he aims his arrows, let them be blunted.

8 Let them be like the snail that dissolves into slime, like the stillborn child who never sees the sun.

9 Sooner than your pots can feel the heat of thorns, whether green or ablaze, may he sweep them away!

10 The righteous will rejoice when he sees the vengeance; he will bathe his feet in the blood of the wicked.

11 Mankind will say, "Surely there is a reward for the righteous; surely there is a God who judges on earth."

Judge of Judges

I am appalled, my God, over the injustice found in our courts. Too often, I hear that another corrupt judge has been removed. I feel angry and frustrated. How long will this go on?

For the wicked judge, "justice" depends on the flow of money, not on upholding the law. For family and friends, evil judges close their eyes, excuse any crime, and declare verdicts in their favor. How can the innocent find justice?

Judges distort justice in their corrupt thinking. They carefully learn ways to twist the law to benefit those they favor. They explain away any injustice as a point of law.

God, I feel so helpless! I am an ordinary citizen who has never been in a trial. Nevertheless, the pain of injustice batters my soul, so I bring this need to You.

Evil judges caught in the act are the ones I hear about. Because they have been removed, they can no longer harm us. However, others continue to inflict pain on the innocent and corrupt our legal system. Please, Judge of all the earth, rip them out of their courtrooms. Pull the teeth of their judicial power and their corrupt influence. Drain away their arrogance and contempt for the law as quickly as a flash flood disappears. Don't allow them to believe that their partiality is justified. Sweep them away in a firestorm.

After suffering under the tyranny of unjust judges, we cry for relief. When You give us freedom from them, we will rejoice over Your mercies. We will bow before You and acknowledge that only You can reward us with righteous judges.

By the power of the Holy Spirit, touch the hearts of all our judges. Bring them to recognize their accountability to You. Show them that You are their Judge.

Psalm 59

1 Deliver me from my enemies, O my God; protect me from those who rise up against me;

2 deliver me from those who work evil, and save me from bloodthirsty men.

3 For behold, they lie in wait for my life; fierce men stir up strife against me. For no transgression or sin of mine, O Lord,

4 for no fault of mine, they run and make ready. Awake, come to meet me, and see!

5 You, Lord God of hosts, are God of Israel. Rouse yourself to punish all the nations; spare none of those who treacherously plot evil.

Selah

6 Each evening they come back, howling like dogs and prowling about the city.

7 There they are, bellowing with their mouths with swords in their lips—for "Who," they think, "will hear us?"

8 But you, O Lord, laugh at them; you hold all the nations in derision.

9 O my Strength, I will watch for you, for you, O God, are my fortress.

10 My God in his steadfast love will meet me; God will let me look in triumph on my enemies.

11 Kill them not, lest my people forget; make them totter by your power and bring them down, O Lord, our shield!

12 For the sin of their mouths, the words of their lips, let them be trapped in their pride. For the cursing and lies that they utter,

Media Frenzy

Help, Lord! Deliver me from this chaos.

Yesterday I lived a quiet, anonymous life. Today a media frenzy focuses on me. If I were a celebrity, a politician, or a criminal, I could understand. That's not me. I'm not famous, so why do I have trucks parked along the street and people camped around my house?

People who lust for rumors examine my past. They forge lies from events long forgotten. They use the lies to explain who I am to their audience. Why should anyone care?

Lord, those who listen to the lies and believe them are no less guilty than the ones who gather the gossip. Please show them how wrong they are. If they ignore the liars, the lies would stop.

Father, I'm afraid. The clicking cameras follow me to the grocery store and the post office. If I try to visit friends, faceless people ambush me. At night, they prowl around the edges of my property. Even though I close my windows and pull down my blinds, I hear their rude, insulting remarks. They act like a pack of wild dogs, snarling and prowling as they harass their prey.

If I had to face these scavengers alone, I might fall to them, but I am not alone. Thank You, oh Lord God of Hosts, that You surround me. You are my stronghold. I focus on You as I pray for strength and wisdom to display Your glory. I call on reinforcements as I ask my friends to stand in prayer with me.

With Your constant guidance, I will not be prey for these scavengers; instead I will pray for them. Do not kill them, because others will simply rise in their place. Instead, by Your great power, bring them down from their persuasive positions and turn them into homeless wanderers. Let them be caught in their own lies. Let their curses fall on their own heads. Then when they look for new prey, let their prowling be futile. Let them find nothing as small as a single scrap to satisfy their lust for lies. In their emptiness, let them seek You.

This media frenzy may disrupt my normal activities, but it cannot separate You from me. In my house, I sing of Your strength. I commit my ways to You at night and proclaim Your faithful love when I awake. In all of these troubles, You give me peace, my faithful God. I will always sing Your praises.

13 consume them in wrath; consume them till they are no more, that they may know that God rules over Jacob to the ends of the earth.

Selah

14 Each evening they come back, howling like dogs and prowling about the city.

15 They wander about for food and growl if they do not get their fill.

16 But I will sing of your strength; I will sing aloud of your steadfast love in the morning. For you have been to me a fortress and a refuge in the day of my distress.

17 O my Strength, I will sing praises to you, for you, O God, are my fortress, the God who shows me steadfast love.

My Prayer

Psalm 60

1 O God, you have rejected us, broken our defenses; you have been angry; oh, restore us.

2 You have made the land to quake; you have torn it open; repair its breaches, for it totters.

3 You have made your people see hard things; you have given us wine to drink that made us stagger.

4 You have set up a banner for those who fear you, that they may flee to it from the bow.

Selah

5 That your beloved ones may be delivered, give salvation by your right hand and answer us!

6 God has spoken in his holiness: "With exultation I will divide up Shechem and portion out the Vale of Succoth.

7 Gilead is mine; Manasseh is mine; Ephraim is my helmet; Judah is my scepter.

8 Moab is my washbasin; upon Edom I cast my shoe; over Philistia I shout in triumph."

9 Who will bring me to the fortified city? Who will lead me to Edom?

10 Have you not rejected us, O God? You do not go forth, O God, with our armies.

11 Oh, grant us help against the foe, for vain is the salvation of man!

12 With God we shall do valiantly; it is he who will tread down our foes.

BATTLE STRATEGY

God Almighty, Your hand of judgment presses on our nation: violent storms destroy, enemy attacks succeed, and our economy slows to a crawl. These crises come from You. You shred the fabric of our lives. You grieve us with the pain and destruction.

That our crises come from You gives me hope. Only the One who controls the weather can calm the storms. You can stir up our enemies or cause them to live in peace with us. Since only You have the power to destroy us, You are the only One who can restore us.

I ask you to restore us, even though we do not deserve it. We deserve to be punished because we reject You. I ask that You cause our crises to soften hearts and draw sinners to You.

You delight in rewarding obedience, not in punishing rebellion. Even in our rebellion You love us too much to leave us separated from You. You set up a banner of salvation in Jesus Christ, Your Son. Oh that all might flee to Him for safety!

Holy God, You declare to the kingdoms of creation that the children of Israel belong to You. In this present age, You also call out many people from the nations and add them to Your church. Your strategy is to bring strangers into Your kingdom as You triumph over Your enemies. Our nation seems to be insensible to Your call.

Father, we desire the collapse of walls around the hearts of those who fortify themselves against You. Fill our hearts with a passion to pray, to love, and to serve. Lead us in the fight for our neighbors' souls. The battle is Yours, Lord. By Your judgments, You replace our nation's smug self-satisfaction with fear and uncertainty. By Your power, You conquer Your enemies.

With You commanding the army of the Lord, we will win these battles. Our shouts of victory will praise You for Your strategy of judgment and love.

Psalm 61

1. Hear my cry, O God, listen to my prayer;

2. from the end of the earth I call to you when my heart is faint. Lead me to the rock that is higher than I,

3. for you have been my refuge, a strong tower against the enemy.

4. Let me dwell in your tent forever! Let me take refuge under the shelter of your wings!

Selah

5. For you, O God, have heard my vows; you have given me the heritage of those who fear your name.

6. Prolong the life of the king; may his years endure to all generations!

7. May he be enthroned forever before God; appoint steadfast love and faithfulness to watch over him!

8. So will I ever sing praises to your name, as I perform my vows day after day.

Graduation Day

Father, I approach You with a sense of urgency. I feel that my time on earth will soon end. My heart faints in weariness. My body weakens by the day. I know the time comes soon when You will release me from this worn-out tent.

What a marvelous day that will be. You will come to lead me to a higher place. No longer will I fight in the thickest part of the battle. Here in the battle, You protect me from my enemies. You are my strong tower, refreshing me as I pour out my strength. Nevertheless, the day will come when no enemy can reach me. I will fight no longer. Instead, I will shelter under the feathers of Your wings. I will serve with greater joy, yet never feel weary. My childhood studies completed, I will graduate into full service in Your House.

My graduation day. New horizons. Eternity unfolds. Added to these blessings, I have those who have gone before me to share that glorious day. Generations of grandmothers and grandfathers will be ready to celebrate with me when I arrive. What a wonderful graduation gift.

For the time I have left in this world, Father, I ask a great favor. Would You give a measure of stability to our government and of peace to our world? Yes, I am selfish in my request. You have blessed me with such a marvelous family and wonderful friends. Would You please grant me a time of green pastures and still waters? Would You allow me to enjoy my time with them for just a little longer?

Whether my last days here are spent in peace or in chaos, whether they be many days or few, I will sing praises to your Name. Then when You release me from this life and I graduate into a heavenly one, I will sing Your praises *forever*. You are always worthy of all praise.

Psalm 62

1 For God alone my soul waits in silence; from him comes my salvation.

2 He only is my rock and my salvation, my fortress; I shall not be greatly shaken.

3 How long will all of you attack a man to batter him, like a leaning wall, a tottering fence?

4 They only plan to thrust him down from his high position. They take pleasure in falsehood. They bless with their mouths, but inwardly they curse.

Selah

5 For God alone, O my soul, wait in silence, for my hope is from him.

6 He only is my rock and my salvation, my fortress; I shall not be shaken.

7 On God rests my salvation and my glory; my mighty rock, my refuge is God.

8 Trust in him at all times, O people; pour out your heart before him; God is a refuge for us.

Selah

9 Those of low estate are but a breath; those of high estate are a delusion; in the balances they go up; they are together lighter than a breath.

10 Put no trust in extortion; set no vain hopes on robbery; if riches increase, set not your heart on them.

Battered by Life

Good morning, God. I join You in this early morning quiet. I slow my thoughts. Dropping from my mind are distractions that wait to claim me when I leave. In silence, I bow before You. I stand here, the attitudes and activities of my life laid out before You.

You know well my battle with sin. Your Son is the one who received my punishment for it. I have such peace knowing that the death verdict no longer applies to me. Instead of judging me, you are my rock, my salvation, and my fortress. Sudden changes in my life, trials, or temptations may surprise me, but I will not be shaken because I have peace with You.

So why do I feel attacked—like a concrete slab battered by a jackhammer? Where are the days of peace and tranquility for which I long? Why do my days feel chaotic? They drive me to You as I seek refuge. You quiet my soul when I seek You in silence.

Since You know me so thoroughly, I can safely open my heart to You. I pour out my thoughts, fears, and uncertainties. I trust You with everything. How wonderful to give You all my burdens!

Thank You for reminding me that this stage of life is as brief as a single breath. So many of the things that I think are enormous problems are only shams—false fronts and phony concerns meant to drive a wedge between us. You hold me steady against them all. I need You to assure me, again, that all power belongs to You. Though battered by life, I find all my rest in You.

11 Once God has spoken; twice have I heard this: that power belongs to God,

12 and that to you, O Lord, belongs steadfast love. For you will render to a man according to his work.

My Prayer

Psalm 63

1. O God, you are my God; earnestly I seek you; my soul thirsts for you; my flesh faints for you, as in a dry and weary land where there is no water.

2. So I have looked upon you in the sanctuary, beholding your power and glory.

3. Because your steadfast love is better than life, my lips will praise you.

4. So I will bless you as long as I live; in your name I will lift up my hands.

5. My soul will be satisfied as with fat and rich food, and my mouth will praise you with joyful lips,

6. when I remember you upon my bed, and meditate on you in the watches of the night;

7. for you have been my help, and in the shadow of your wings I will sing for joy.

8. My soul clings to you; your right hand upholds me.

9. But those who seek to destroy my life shall go down into the depths of the earth;

10. they shall be given over to the power of the sword; they shall be a portion for jackals.

11. But the king shall rejoice in God; all who swear by him shall exult, for the mouths of liars will be stopped.

Living in the Land of Liars

Father, I live in the land of liars. Sometimes with subtlety, often stridently, people say, "There is no god." This preposterous idea astonishes me. I experience life with You so intimately that I cannot imagine living without You.

Just as my body thirsts for water, my soul thirsts for You. I earnestly seek to live in Your presence. In this cultural wasteland, I work hard to resist the lies I hear and vow to abide in You. If I drift along with everyone else, I find myself feeling separated from You.

Instead of drifting, I discipline myself to focus on You. I join other Christians to worship You at church. Together we hold You in the highest regard, confessing that You are God Almighty, worthy to be praised. We lift our hands and bow our hearts in worship.

Alone, I read the Bible, filling my soul with rich food. I savor the beauty and truth within its pages as I read it aloud. I meditate on Your words of life. I memorize passages and praise You as I repeat them.

Even in the middle of the night, I eagerly seek You. I sing praise songs in my heart. I meditate on the Bible passages that I have stored in my memory. I talk to You and I listen to the Holy Spirit. No time or place exists that we cannot be together.

In this dangerous land of liars, You protect me. Your right hand safely holds me. I rest in the shadow of Your wings.

The liars delude themselves and seek to destroy my joy in You. (I was one of them until You gave me new life.) These liars are without life. They would rather face the sword of judgment than to confess that You are God. They cling to their rejection of You even as it destroys them.

Nevertheless, all who confess that forgiveness of sins can be found only in Jesus Christ will see the day when You stop the lies. King Jesus will claim His throne and all the liars will open their mouths to confess, "Jesus Christ is Lord." Though the words are bitter in their mouths, they will acknowledge that You are God. Your children, however, will glory with joy and gladness to see the collapse of the land of liars.

Psalm 64

1. Hear my voice, O God, in my complaint; preserve my life from dread of the enemy.
2. Hide me from the secret plots of the wicked, from the throng of evildoers,
3. who whet their tongues like swords, who aim bitter words like arrows,
4. shooting from ambush at the blameless, shooting at him suddenly and without fear.
5. They hold fast to their evil purpose; they talk of laying snares secretly, thinking, who can see them?
6. They search out injustice, saying, "We have accomplished a diligent search." For the inward mind and heart of a man are deep!
7. But God shoots his arrow at them; they are wounded suddenly.
8. They are brought to ruin, with their own tongues turned against them; all who see them will wag their heads.
9. Then all mankind fears; they tell what God has brought about and ponder what he has done.
10. Let the righteous one rejoice in the Lord and take refuge in him! Let all the upright in heart exult!

Conspiracy Schemes

Lord, after seeing it so many times, I should recognize the character assassinations that crop up during every election campaign cycle. Nevertheless, it usually takes me by surprise. I dread the bombardment of TV ads, radio spots, and candidate mail. Every year I feel dismayed by the degree to which they become more and more negative.

Cunning people in "public relations" jobs sharpen their tongues like swords. They meet, conspire, and declare, "We have the perfect plan!" The "spin doctors" bait their traps with bits of truth. They attempt to lure the voters into hidden snares. They seek to grab people's attention and cover their thoughts with verbal graffiti. By Your power, I stay alert, dodging the ambushes that lure me away from You and from the peace that reigns in my heart.

The whole thing disgusts me. These campaign specialists conspire with each other; I want to conspire with You. Hear my prayer, oh Lord.

Protect the candidates from slander and exaggeration. Attack those who plot injustice, using their own words against them, bringing them to ruin. Shake them away from their schemes with such intense force that they turn to You in surrender.

Bring fear into the hearts of the wicked as they consider the bitter harvest of their work. Sow the seeds of repentance within them so that they find salvation in Jesus. Then all the righteous will rejoice in You. All the upright in heart will praise You.

Psalm 65

1 Praise is due to you, O God, in Zion, and to you shall vows be performed.

2 O you who hears prayer, to you shall all flesh come.

3 When iniquities prevail against me, you atone for our transgressions.

4 Blessed is the one you choose and bring near, to dwell in your courts! We shall be satisfied with the goodness of your house, the holiness of your temple!

5 By awesome deeds you answer us with righteousness, O God of our salvation, the hope of all the ends of the earth and of the farthest seas;

6 the one who by his strength established the mountains, being girded with might;

7 who stills the roaring of the seas, the roaring of their waves, the tumult of the peoples,

8 so that those who dwell at the ends of the earth are in awe at your signs. You make the going out of the morning and the evening to shout for joy.

9 You visit the earth and water it; you greatly enrich it; the river of God is full of water; you provide their grain, for so you have prepared it.

10 You water its furrows abundantly, settling its ridges, softening it with showers, and blessing its growth.

11 You crown the year with your bounty; your wagon tracks overflow with abundance.

Crowned with Your Bounty

Praise is always due to You, our God. You draw us to You and listen to our prayers. You provided a Sacrifice to pay for our sins. You choose us to be the home of Your Holy Spirit—a living temple for You. You satisfy us by allowing us to live in Your holy presence. Your salvation is the answer to our every need. You are the hope of everyone, even to the ends of the earth and the most distant seas.

How can it be any other way, since You created the world? Over the eons, You move the mountains into place. You sculpt the earth into landscapes of astonishing beauty.

The oceans respond to Your commands. In some places, they murmur quietly, swishing softly onto the sand. On other shores, they pound upon the rocks, roaring up to the beach like a freight train in the night.

In the same way, You control the tumult of the nations. You hush one nation's strident complaints while another's grievance becomes the flashpoint for war. The nations' futures are in Your hands. Open their citizens' eyes so that they revere Your power. From lands where morning dawns to those where evening fades, call forth songs of joy in those who trust You.

Just as You mold the mountains and move the nations, so too do You control the cycle of the seasons and set the fertility of the earth. In their proper time, You water the earth, sending spring storms and summer showers. (The farmer harrows his field and plants his seeds uselessly unless You soften the soil with showers and bless the plants with growth.) You bless the wild places too, clothing the hills with green grasses and blooming flowers until the desert sings for joy in its richest robes.

Lest we take for granted the mystery of Your presence, You give us the beauty of the earth and the pleasure of the seasons, and You crown the year with Your harvest bounty. The wagons at harvest overflow with abundance. You delight in providing food for the flocks. You lavishly give us reasons to rejoice in You.

Oh Father, so often we do take every blessing—from Your eternal presence to the short-lived crust of bread on the table—for granted. Give us humble, grateful hearts so that we do not simply celebrate a Thanksgiving Day. Instead show us the way to rejoice with a thankful life. Let us shout and sing for joy as we praise You forever because You crown us with Your bounty.

12 The pastures of the wilderness overflow, the hills gird themselves with joy,

13 the meadows clothe themselves with flocks, the valleys deck themselves with grain, they shout and sing together for joy.

My Prayer

Psalm 66

1 Shout for joy to God, all the earth;

2 sing the glory of his name; give to him glorious praise!

3 Say to God, "How awesome are your deeds! So great is your power that your enemies come cringing to you.

4 All the earth worships you and sings praises to you; they sing praises to your name."

Selah

5 Come and see what God has done: he is awesome in his deeds toward the children of man.

6 He turned the sea into dry land; they passed through the river on foot. There did we rejoice in him,

7 who rules by his might forever, whose eyes keep watch on the nations— let not the rebellious exalt themselves.

Selah

8 Bless our God, O peoples; let the sound of his praise be heard,

9 who has kept our soul among the living and has not let our feet slip.

10 For you, O God, have tested us; you have tried us as silver is tried.

11 You brought us into the net; you laid a crushing burden on our backs;

12 you let men ride over our heads; we went through fire and through water; yet you have brought us out to a place of abundance.

13 I will come into your house with burnt offerings; I will perform my vows to you,

Make His Praise Glorious

This is a day of exuberant praise. I shout for joy, oh God of all creation. I sing the glory of Your Name. You do exceedingly more than I could imagine.

By calling back to life the crucified Christ, You caused all Your enemies to cringe before You. You destroyed the power of death. The heavens and the earth sing praises to Your Name.

For me, You dried the sea of righteous judgment. For me, You bridged the gap between my rebellion and Your holiness. Your firstborn Son died in my place. Because I crossed the bridge You built for me, I rejoice that You live in my heart forever.

Yes, because of Your great love, I, who was one of the walking dead, *live*. I praise You, for Your love securely holds me. I can never slip back into that state of existence.

By the trials and tests You bring into my life, I see that You care for me. You love me too much to leave me in my sinful rags and my habits of rebellion. I often think that the fires and the floods will crush me. Yet when the flames die and when the water drains, I find myself purified, set free from sinful habits and living life more abundantly. For this I greatly praise You.

I remember the promises I made when I was in trouble. You know I vowed from my heart to keep these commitments. I will give You the sacrifice of praise and worship. I will present incense: my prayers of thanksgiving. I will tell what You have done everywhere You send me. I will proclaim Your wonderful deeds.

Because I heard Your call to repent and I wanted You more than I wanted my sinful existence, You listened to my prayer of confession. Since that day, You have poured out Your steadfast love on me. I want to live a life that makes Your praise glorious.

14 that which my lips uttered and my mouth promised when I was in trouble.

15 I will offer to you burnt offerings of fattened animals, with the smoke of the sacrifice of rams; I will make an offering of bulls and goats.

Selah

16 Come and hear, all you who fear God, and I will tell what he has done for my soul.

17 I cried to him with my mouth, and high praise was on my tongue.

18 If I had cherished iniquity in my heart, the Lord would not have listened.

19 But truly God has listened; he has attended to the voice of my prayer.

20 Blessed be God, because he has not rejected my prayer or removed his steadfast love from me!

My Prayer

Psalm 67

1 May God be gracious to us and bless us and make his face to shine upon us,

Selah

2 that your way may be known on earth, your saving power among all nations.

3 Let the peoples praise you, O God; let all the peoples praise you!

4 Let the nations be glad and sing for joy, for you judge the peoples with equity and guide the nations upon earth.

Selah

5 Let the peoples praise you, O God; let all the peoples praise you!

6 The earth has yielded its increase; God, our God, shall bless us.

7 God shall bless us; let all the ends of the earth fear him!

A Blessing from Israel

Adonai, Lord God of Israel, before that nation put one foot on the land that You promised them, You taught Aaron and his sons a blessing to be spoken over the people. On a regular basis, Your priests put Your Name upon the nation of Israel. As a priest under the New Covenant, I speak this blessing over the renewed nation of Israel:

"Adonai bless you and keep you;

Adonai make His face to shine upon you and be gracious to you;

Adonai lift up His countenance upon you and give you peace." (Num. 6:24–26)

Lord God of Israel, I speak this blessing upon Your chosen people so that You will bless them. That tiny nation, so far from the power centers of this world, displays Your awesome power to all the nations. By Your power alone, You called it into existence. You maintain it day by day. For this, Oh Lord, all Your people praise You.

Because You chose Israel long ago and bless them still today, people from every land and language can rejoice. From Israel of old, you sent Jesus to be born the Son of David. By His sacrifice, He created peace with You and brings justice for all.

You will send this same Jesus to modern Israel. He will return as King of kings. He will judge the people of the earth with fairness. He will rule the nations of the world with a rod of iron. With great rejoicing, Your people will praise You.

Yet You have planned a greater day—a harvest day—when all the nations of the earth will find their rebellion has an end. On that day, all Your enemies will die. Only those who love and fear You will remain. How they will praise You on that day! Yes, Adonai, all creation will praise You.

Psalm 68:1–14

1 God shall arise, his enemies shall be scattered; and those who hate him shall flee before him!

2 As smoke is driven away, so you shall drive them away; as wax melts before fire, so the wicked shall perish before God!

3 But the righteous shall be glad; they shall exult before God; they shall be jubilant with joy!

4 Sing to God, sing praises to his name; lift up a song to him who rides through the deserts; his name is the Lord; exult before him!

5 Father of the fatherless and protector of widows is God in his holy habitation.

6 God settles the solitary in a home; he leads out the prisoners to prosperity, but the rebellious dwell in a parched land.

7 O God, when you went out before your people, when you marched through the wilderness,

Selah

8 the earth quaked, the heavens poured down rain, before God, the One of Sinai, before God, the God of Israel.

9 Rain in abundance, O God, you shed abroad; you restored your inheritance as it languished;

10 your flock found a dwelling in it; in your goodness, O God, you provided for the needy.

11 The Lord gives the word; the women who announce the news are a great host:

12 "The kings of the armies—they flee, they flee!" The women at home divide the spoil—

An Attack of Loneliness

Arise, oh God. Scatter my enemies. Like a hundred little imps, the army of loneliness attacks me. Cause them to flee before You. Blow them away as wind scatters smoke. Melt their strength like wax in a flame. Destroy this evil army and I will be jubilant with joy.

I won't wait to see this happen before I sing Your praise. I confidently call upon You. You are the Lord God Almighty. You come quickly to my rescue, though I travel in a waterless wasteland. You swiftly come to aid me.

I trust You, Father, for I remember the way You rescued the Israelites as they slaved for the Egyptians. You moved heaven and earth to settle them in the Land of Promise. In Your goodness, You created a powerful nation from lonely slaves.

Loneliness isolates me from You and from others. The army of loneliness drains my strength. I will remember You and resist!

Hear the orphans cry, "My father abandoned me. My mother rejected me. I am alone!"

In response You proclaim, "I Am father to the fatherless. I do not reject you. Come to me, my child."

The widow exclaims, "My husband is gone! Who will love me? Who will share my joy and comfort me in my sorrows? I am all alone."

Tenderly You say, "I will protect you and be your husband. I will multiply your joys and bear your burdens. Lay your head on my shoulder, beloved."

The solitary man says in his heart, "Where is my wife, my partner in life? My footsteps echo in this empty house. Why must I live alone?"

With mercy You speak. "I set the lonely in families. I create homes in houses. No one who finds Me lives alone. Seek Me first; I will share My life with you."

The prisoner, alone in his sterile cell, cries out, "My life is over. I have nothing. No one cares if I live or die."

"Lies!" You tell him. "Only lies. Steel bars and cement walls cannot separate Me from you. The things you lost have no eternal value. Seek Me with all your heart and I will give you life without end and wealth that will last forever."

13 though you men lie among the sheepfolds—the wings of a dove covered with silver, its pinions with shimmering gold.

14 When the Almighty scatters kings there, let snow fall on Zalmon.

Day after day, You defend each of us from the attack of loneliness. You force our enemies to flee. Women rejoice and spread the good news. Men find their treasure in You. You break the drought of loneliness. You refresh us. Loneliness flees and we find sweet companionship with You. We praise You, God of all comfort, The One Who Never Leaves Me Alone.

Psalm 68:15–35

15 O mountain of God, mountain of Bashan; O many-peaked mountain, mountain of Bashan!

16 Why do you look with hatred, O many-peaked mountain, at the mount that God desired for his abode, yes, where the Lord will dwell forever?

17 The chariots of God are twice ten thousand, thousands upon thousands; the Lord is among them; Sinai is now in the sanctuary.

18 You ascended on high, leading a host of captives in your train and receiving gifts among men, even among the rebellious, that the Lord God may dwell there.

19 Blessed be the Lord, who daily bears us up; God is our salvation.

Selah

20 Our God is a God of salvation, and to God, the Lord, belong deliverances from death.

21 But God will strike the heads of his enemies, the hairy crown of him who walks in his guilty ways.

22 The Lord said, "I will bring them back from Bashan, I will bring them back from the depths of the sea,

23 that you may strike your feet in their blood, that the tongues of your dogs may have their portion from the foe."

24 Your procession is seen, O God, the procession of my God, my King, into the sanctuary—

25 the singers in front, the musicians last, between them virgins playing tambourines:

26 "Bless God in the great congregation, the Lord, O you who are of Israel's fountain!"

Victory Parade

Where are the arrogant nations who looked on You with hatred? What became of the mighty hosts of humanity who despised the simple carpenter, the Son of Mary? The Roman Empire and the Jewish kingdom that nailed You to the cross are gone.

You, however—Jesus Christ, Son of the Living God—are alive forever. Death could not hold You. The grave could not keep You. Surrounded by a myriad of angels, You ascended to the highest heaven. You brought with You a rejoicing host of captives set free, prisoners freed from the death camp. With You came the spoils of war: life instead of death, freedom from sin instead of rebellion, and power over our enemies instead of helplessness.

You are worthy of all our praise, Lord. You cleansed us from sin and remove our guilt. Father God, You saved us by pouring out Your wrath on Jesus. Because You died in my place, Jesus, You delivered me from death.

You won the war and vanquished the rebellious, yet earthly battles remain to be fought. The cup of Your wrath against those who continue to walk in their rebellious ways is not yet full. Therefore, we fight until the time for their judgment arrives.

On that day, You will resurrect—from the land and the seas—the guilty ones to face their crimes. As they wait to hear the details of their sentences, they will see an extraordinary victory parade. You will lead it, King of kings and Lord of lords.

As You take Your throne, the heavenly choir will pass before You. "Worthy are You to receive glory and honor and power," they will sing. The band will play while virgins dance to the sound of tambourines. Your sons and daughters will parade past You. The weakest ones will lead the procession and the strongest ones will follow them.

On that day, from Your throne You will speak. The power of Your rebuke will remove the aggressive bulls, destroying those who lust to enslave others. You will scatter—with a single word—those who delight in war. Then, every nation from the greatest empire to the lowliest vassal state will bring You tribute.

Shall we wait until that day to sing Your praises? Shall we keep quiet so that many will not hear of You until the victory procession passes before them? No! Today is the day of salvation. Today You ride in the heavens,

27 There is Benjamin, the least of them, in the lead, the princes of Judah in their throng, the princes of Zebulun, the princes of Naphtali.

28 Summon your power, O God, the power, O God, by which you have worked for us.

29 Because of your temple at Jerusalem kings shall bear gifts to you.

30 Rebuke the beasts that dwell among the reeds, the herd of bulls with the calves of the peoples. Trample underfoot those who lust after tribute; scatter the peoples who delight in war.

31 Nobles shall come from Egypt; Cush shall hasten to stretch out her hands to God.

32 O kingdoms of the earth, sing to God; sing praises to the Lord,

Selah

33 to him who rides in the heavens, the ancient heavens; behold, he sends out his voice, his mighty voice.

34 Ascribe power to God, whose majesty is over Israel, and whose power is in the skies.

35 Awesome is God from his sanctuary; the God of Israel—he is the one who gives power and strength to his people.

Blessed be God!

the highest heavens, speaking peace to rebels on earth. You, our majestic, awesome God, send out Your mighty voice across the earth to give hope to sinners. You bought the victory over sin with Your blood. You desire that all might share in it and walk in the victory parade. May all creation in heaven and earth rejoice that You are the Victorious One.

Psalm 69:1–15

1   Save me, O God! For the waters have come up to my neck.

2   I sink in deep mire, where there is no foothold; I have come into deep waters, and the flood sweeps over me.

3   I am weary with my crying out; my throat is parched. My eyes grow dim with waiting for my God.

4   More in number than the hairs of my head are those who hate me without cause; mighty are those who would destroy me, those who attack me with lies. What I did not steal must I now restore?

5   O God, you know my folly; the wrongs I have done are not hidden from you.

6   Let not those who hope in you be put to shame through me, O Lord God of hosts; let not those who seek you be brought to dishonor through me, O God of Israel.

7   For it is for your sake that I have borne reproach, that dishonor has covered my face.

8   I have become a stranger to my brothers, an alien to my mother's sons.

9   For zeal for your house has consumed me, and the reproaches of those who reproach you have fallen on me.

10 When I wept and humbled my soul with fasting, it became my reproach.

11 When I made sackcloth my clothing, I became a byword to them.

12 I am the talk of those who sit in the gate, and the drunkards make songs about me.

Prophet's Prayer

Who will believe the vision You have given me? You chose a nobody and seared Your Living Word on my heart. I *must* proclaim the warning. The words fly off my tongue. They flow from the end of my pen. A few people listen. I had hoped that everyone else would ignore me. What a naïve daydream!

I feel as if I'd tried to cross a river at a shallow ford only to fall into a deep hole. A flood of scorn sweeps over me. Nevertheless, I publish Your words until my throat parches and my hand cramps. When will you say, "Enough" and come to my rescue?

From the waves of verbal abuse and scorn coming at me, I feel like I stand alone pushing back the tide. Even the tax people investigate me. Must I pay them what I never owed?

God, You know that I am far from perfect. If my enemies dig deeply enough, they will find my follies and my sins. By now, I have no reputation anyway, so they can't hurt me. However, I ask You to protect those who hope in You so that nothing my enemies drag up puts Your children to shame. Do not let those who seek You be brought to dishonor because of something I did.

If not for Your call on my life, I would be an anonymous, invisible nobody. The cost for proclaiming Your message has been reproach, dishonor, and rejection. People identify me so closely with your Word that they want to shoot the messenger. When I speak, they curse me. The words I speak disgust them. They call me a crazy person for speaking them. I am covered with their sarcasm. The mud they sling piles up around me. Every time I open my mouth, I search for the pit of quicksand—a trap set to sink me.

If You had not saved me, the floodwaters of abuse would overwhelm me. You keep me safe when those who feel threatened by Your message want me dead. Thank You for protecting me as You send me. Your great grace rescues me from those who hate me. Some will hear and heed Your message. They will embrace the truth of Your salvation. Thank You for allowing me to deliver the message that brings them life everlasting. That alone makes my weary days worth the price.

13 But as for me, my prayer is to you, O Lord. At an acceptable time, O God, in the abundance of your steadfast love answer me in your saving faithfulness.

14 Deliver me from sinking in the mire; let me be delivered from my enemies and from the deep waters.

15 Let not the flood sweep over me, or the deep swallow me up, or the pit close its mouth over me.

My Prayer

Psalm 69:16–36

16 Answer me, O Lord, for your steadfast love is good; according to your abundant mercy, turn to me.

17 Hide not your face from your servant; for I am in distress; make haste to answer me.

18 Draw near to my soul, redeem me; ransom me because of my enemies!

19 You know my reproach, and my shame and my dishonor; my foes are all known to you.

20 Reproaches have broken my heart, so that I am in despair. I looked for pity, but there was none, and for comforters, but I found none.

21 They gave me poison for food, and for my thirst they gave me sour wine to drink.

22 Let their own table before them become a snare; and when they are at peace, let it become a trap.

23 Let their eyes be darkened, so that they cannot see, and make their loins tremble continually.

24 Pour out your indignation upon them, and let your burning anger overtake them.

25 May their camp be a desolation; let no one dwell in their tents.

26 For they persecute him whom you have struck down, and they recount the pain of those you have wounded.

27 Add to them punishment upon punishment; may they have no acquittal from you.

28 Let them be blotted out of the book of the living; let them not be enrolled among the righteous.

TOUGH LOVE

Father, what is happening? Devastation converges on me from every direction. I did not expect this. When I turned away from my sins, I expected my life to get better, not worse.

You changed me that day I turned to You. You opened my eyes, drew me into Your steadfast love, and saturated me with Your abundant mercy. You redeemed me by the blood of Jesus. The excitement had me high-fiving the world.

Yet my family and friends' reactions to my salvation bring me to despair. You know that before You saved me I had the same lifestyle they have now. I cared nothing for honor and boasted of living a shameful life. They continue living that way, rejecting You and my new lifestyle. My family won't even speak to me.

What can I do? My heart is broken. Why can they not understand what an amazing God You are? I don't understand.

I tried telling a few people how hurt I am by this rejection. I found no comforters, no one to take pity on me and show me the best way to respond. Instead, they fed me pious platitudes.

I can't reach my family, God, but You can. Do to them the same things that brought me to You. Trap them when they sit down to eat and least expect it. When they feel peaceful, show them the emptiness of their lives. Sow fear in their hearts in times of uncertainty. Give them a view of their day of judgment. Let them see Your burning anger that is set to overtake them. Show them that when they reject Your love, they are turning their backs on Jesus' sacrifice. Because they turn their backs on Jesus, You will add punishment to punishment, separating them forever from Your children who live in righteousness.

When I understood the horror of hell, I answered Your call. Now pain grips my heart for the future facing the ones I love. Save my family, God. That would be so awesome.

While I wait, I will praise You even as I grieve for my family and friends. At the same time, I will confess that You are The God Who Saves. I will find Christian brothers and sisters who will pray with me for my family's salvation. You will revive my heart as I trust in You.

29 But I am afflicted and in pain; let your salvation, O God, set me on high!

30 I will praise the name of God with a song; I will magnify him with thanksgiving.

31 This will please the Lord more than an ox or a bull with horns and hoofs.

32 When the humble see it they will be glad; you who seek God, let your hearts revive.

33 For the Lord hears the needy and does not despise his own people who are prisoners.

34 Let heaven and earth praise him, the seas and everything that moves in them.

35 For God will save Zion and build up the cities of Judah, and people shall dwell there and possess it;

36 the offspring of his servants shall inherit it, and those who love his name shall dwell in it.

On the days I feel cast down, I will anticipate—like a child for Christmas Day—the day each member of my family comes to put their trust in You. I will look forward to the way heaven and earth rejoice as their souls enter Your kingdom. When my physical family joins my spiritual family, we will all join to sing Your praises. Halleluiah!

Psalm 70

1 Make haste, O God, to deliver me! O Lord, make haste to help me!

2 Let them be put to shame and confusion who seek my life! Let them be turned back and brought to dishonor who desire my hurt!

3 Let them turn back because of their shame who say, "Aha, Aha!"

4 May all who seek you rejoice and be glad in you! May those who love your salvation say evermore, "God is great!"

5 But I am poor and needy; hasten to me, O God! You are my help and my deliverer; O Lord, do not delay!

Panic Button

Help, Lord!

This crisis blindsided me. I had no idea that I would be caught in such a dangerous situation. Why are these people so hostile? I don't know what to do.

I need Your help now, God. You said You would always be with me, so stand by me. You said You would tell me what to say when I faced an enemy, so give me the words I need. Give me the ability to escape the people who want to destroy me.

Lord, I am frightened and confused, but I trust You to get me through this experience. I need You to rescue me, now. Please do not delay.

By Your power, I will push through. Then I will gladly tell my brothers and sisters how my awesome God rescued me. Together we will praise You saying, "God, You are great."

Psalm 71

1. In you, O Lord, do I take refuge; let me never be put to shame!

2. In your righteousness deliver me and rescue me; incline your ear to me, and save me!

3. Be to me a rock of refuge, to which I may continually come; you have given the command to save me, for you are my rock and my fortress.

4. Rescue me, O my God, from the hand of the wicked, from the grasp of the unjust and cruel man.

5. For you, O Lord, are my hope, my trust, O Lord, from my youth.

6. Upon you I have leaned from before my birth; you are he who took me from my mother's womb. My praise is continually of you.

7. I have been as a portent to many, but you are my strong refuge.

8. My mouth is filled with your praise, and with your glory all the day.

9. Do not cast me off in the time of old age; forsake me not when my strength is spent.

10. For my enemies speak concerning me; those who watch for my life consult together

11. and say, "God has forsaken him; pursue and seize him, for there is none to deliver him."

12. O God, be not far from me; O my God, make haste to help me!

13. May my accusers be put to shame and consumed; with scorn and disgrace may they be covered who seek my hurt.

14. But I will hope continually and will praise you yet more and more.

With Age, My Strength Fails

Father, I continue to seek refuge in You. As I passed through childhood, early adulthood, and middle age, You always heard my requests for help. In times too numerous to count, You rescued and delivered me. You have always been my place of refuge, my fortress of security.

For some reason, I thought my enemies would give up and go away when I grew older. Well, that didn't happen. They have found new ways to attack my trust in You: failing health, children's lifestyles, loved ones' deaths, and financial uncertainty. I could easily fall into fear and worry and stay there. That's not going to happen. My short-term memory may be faulty, but sharp and clear are the memories of the way You shepherd me through life.

When I was four, You saved me from being kicked in the head by a cow. When I was five, You carried me through the dark valley of polio. You gave me the gift of salvation when I was nine, shattered the walls of a mental breakdown when I was a teenager, and led me through the wilderness of my marriage. How could I not hope in You when You always prove that I can trust You?

I wish that I could say that I sailed through all my troubles with a cheerful attitude and a peaceful heart. You know the truth about *that*! I am sure that many times people failed to see my faith in You. Nevertheless, You have always been my strong refuge. My mouth is filled with Your praises.

Yet now, when my strength is failing, my enemies watch me like a flock of vultures. They seem to think that You will have no use for me—that You will desert me—now that I can no longer do Your work. How foolish they are, to believe such a lie.

I may have little strength, but I have more time to praise You. I will tell everyone who will listen about Your righteous acts. I will display Your love by my lifestyle. I will talk about salvation through Jesus.

From my birth until today, through godly parents, teachers, mentors, pastors, and friends, You have taught me. You spent years preparing me to pass on to another generation the revelation of who You are. So Lord, even as I grow older and my hair becomes thin and gray, do not forsake me.

With my feet anchored in the promises You have kept, I will face today's challenges with courage. When I look down the road, I see a curve

15 My mouth will tell of your righteous acts, of your deeds of salvation all the day, for their number is past my knowledge.

16 With the mighty deeds of the Lord God I will come; I will remind them of your righteousness, yours alone.

17 O God, from my youth you have taught me, and I still proclaim your wondrous deeds.

18 So even to old age and gray hairs, O God, do not forsake me, until I proclaim your might to another generation, your power to all those to come.

19 Your righteousness, O God, reaches the high heavens. You who have done great things, O God, who is like you?

20 You who have made me see many troubles and calamities will revive me again; from the depths of the earth you will bring me up again.

21 You will increase my greatness and comfort me again.

22 I will also praise you with the harp for your faithfulness, O my God; I will sing praises to you with the lyre, O Holy One of Israel.

23 My lips will shout for joy, when I sing praises to you; my soul also, which you have redeemed.

24 And my tongue will talk of your righteous help all the day long, for they have been put to shame and disappointed who sought to do me hurt.

labeled "death." Even there, I will trust You. Why should I fear when You promise to replace this sin-worn body with a perfect one? You promise to increase my greatness and comfort me. Even in death You will not forsake me.

For eternity, I will praise You. You faithfully keep every promise. Who is like You, oh God?

Psalm 72

1 **G**ive the king your justice, O God, and your righteousness to the royal son!

2 May he judge your people with righteousness, and your poor with justice!

3 Let the mountains bear prosperity for the people, and the hills, in righteousness!

4 May he defend the cause of the poor of the people, give deliverance to the children of the needy, and crush the oppressor!

5 May they fear you while the sun endures, and as long as the moon, throughout all generations!

6 May he be like rain that falls on the mown grass, like showers that water the earth!

7 In his days may the righteous flourish, and peace abound, till the moon be no more!

8 May he have dominion from sea to sea, and from the River to the ends of the earth!

9 May desert tribes bow down before him and his enemies lick the dust!

10 May the kings of Tarshish and of the coastlands render him tribute; may the kings of Sheba and Seba bring gifts!

11 May all kings fall down before him, all nations serve him!

12 For he delivers the needy when he calls, the poor and him who has no helper.

13 He has pity on the weak and the needy, and saves the lives of the needy.

The Coming Kingdom

Lord, twenty-four hours a day, seven days a week, the news media bombards me with reports of man's inhumanity to man. The stories of social injustice and gross immorality breed anger, frustration, and grief in me. My soul yearns for the coming of Your kingdom on earth.

King Jesus, on the day You return to rule with an iron hand, our struggle against injustice will end. Oh Righteous Royal Son, You will bring justice to the poor. You will protect the weak from the oppressive schemes of the powerful. You will crush even the slyest tormenters before anyone can become a victim of their plots.

Your kingdom will bring days of peace and the rule of righteousness for a thousand years. It will thrive so long that the memories of the ruthless despots who rule today will be like forgotten dreams. Your righteous children will prosper; they will flower under Your rule.

Your throne, King Jesus, is already established in Jerusalem. However, You will rule the nations from the Euphrates River to the ends of the earth. Lesser kings may govern, but You will be Lord over them all.

Some rulers will come gladly to rejoice in the peace and prosperity that You bring. They will bring You gifts of thanksgiving, offerings of peace. Others will bring only their fear and resentment. They will bow before You because they fear to lose what little power they have should they refuse. They will see only Your hand restraining their ambitions. Whatever their reasons for coming, all rulers will bow before You. All nations will serve You.

You will be the hero of ordinary people. Those who desire to live a quiet and peaceful life will find their dreams fulfilled. They will no longer fear their neighbor.

People will petition You in their times of need. You will protect the poor, the weak, and all who have no one else to help them. Their own rulers may callously ignore their problems, but You will care for all people.

Righteous people in every nation will enjoy the blessings of Your kingdom. They will praise You, Father, with songs of thanksgiving. They will thank You for sending Your Son to reign.

Oh, how glorious that will be! I yearn to see the day when everyone has abundant food. Instead of images of starving children that I see today, I will see healthy bodies, active minds, and happy laughter abounding

14 From oppression and violence he redeems their life, and precious is their blood in his sight.

15 Long may he live; may gold of Sheba be given to him! May prayer be made for him continually, and blessings invoked for him all the day!

16 May there be abundance of grain in the land; on the tops of the mountains may it wave; may its fruit be like Lebanon; and may people blossom in the cities like the grass of the field!

17 May his name endure forever, his fame continue as long as the sun! May people be blessed in him, all nations call him blessed!

18 Blessed be the Lord, the God of Israel, who alone does wondrous things.

19 Blessed be his glorious name forever; may the whole earth be filled with his glory! Amen and Amen!

20 The prayers of David, the son of Jesse, are ended.

in children around the world. My mother's heart longs for that day to arrive.

Your kingdom, Lord Jesus, is not a return to the Garden of Eden. Not all of humanity will give up its rebellion against You. Nevertheless, those who embrace You as their Lord and Savior will be blessed in You. Many people in every nation will call on Your Name.

Jehovah, God of Israel, only You could accomplish this wondrous thing. You alone can force humanity into a society where social justice thrives. Your invincible power will restrain strong oppressors and the depraved. As Christ reigns for a thousand years, the whole earth will be filled with Your glory. I will rejoice with all who love You. We will sing, "Blessed be Your glorious name forever."

Psalm 73

1. Truly God is good to Israel, to those who are pure in heart.
2. But as for me, my feet had almost stumbled, my steps had nearly slipped.
3. For I was envious of the arrogant when I saw the prosperity of the wicked.
4. For they have no pangs until death; their bodies are fat and sleek.
5. They are not in trouble as others are; they are not stricken like the rest of mankind.
6. Therefore pride is their necklace; violence covers them as a garment.
7. Their eyes swell out through fatness; their hearts overflow with follies.
8. They scoff and speak with malice; loftily they threaten oppression.
9. They set their mouths against the heavens, and their tongue struts through the earth.
10. Therefore his people turn back to them, and find no fault in them.
11. And they say, "How can God know? Is there knowledge in the Most High?"
12. Behold, these are the wicked; always at ease, they increase in riches.
13. All in vain have I kept my heart clean and washed my hands in innocence.
14. For all the day long I have been stricken and rebuked every morning.
15. If I had said, "I will speak thus," I would have betrayed the generation of your children.

Dead-End World

Lord, Your Word says You are good to Your children, to those who are pure in heart. We go around saying, "God is good all the time" to each other.

Yet I sometimes get ambushed by my ordinary definition for the word "good." By this common definition, the wealthy, powerful people get the good things in life. Their prosperity brings them enjoyable, nutritious food. They never need to decide whether to pay the rent or buy a few groceries. They have healthy bodies, straight teeth, and shiny hair. They shop in the best stores and eat in the finest restaurants. They use their money to increase their wealth. Everything seems to go their way.

Occasionally I will see one of these wealthy people. They wear their pride like a glittering necklace. Many of them believe that all of these good things came to them because they worked hard for it. They smugly assert that they are self-made millionaires.

Others take pride in owning all the things that money can buy. They buy only the latest, the greatest, the best. They feel happy only when all the eyes around them shine with envy.

These arrogant people have one thing in common. Their world revolves around them. These self-centered people have hearts overflowing with folly. They treat everyone with contempt. They threaten anyone who stands in their way. Even You, God, are not exempt from their callous disregard.

I see their pleasurable lifestyle. I think about the freedom from daily struggles that their wealth brings. I compare their life to mine. It's not a pretty picture. I have a body exhausted from work, continual demands for money from my family, and a houseful of hungry children to feed.

God, I feel angry and resentful that I must work hard every day to put a little food on our table. Keeping a roof over our head takes much of my energy. Sometimes I ask myself if I made the right decision when I decided to follow You. Would my life be easier if I tried to live the "good" life?

So I ask You, have I made the right decision? Is obeying You more important than providing a life of comfort and ease for my family? Lord, I come to You for answers. Weariness and bitter tears assault me. Speak comfort to me.

Sitting here in Your sanctuary, Your Spirit reminds me that only You are good. Good in the sense of pure. Good in the sense of desirable. Good in the sense of holy.

16 But when I thought how to understand this, it seemed to me a wearisome task,

17 until I went into the sanctuary of God; then I discerned their end.

18 Truly you set them in slippery places; you make them fall to ruin.

19 How they are destroyed in a moment, swept away utterly by terrors!

20 Like a dream when one awakes, O Lord, when you rouse yourself, you despise them as phantoms.

21 When my soul was embittered, when I was pricked in heart,

22 I was brutish and ignorant; I was like a beast toward you.

23 Nevertheless, I am continually with you; you hold my right hand.

24 You guide me with your counsel, and afterward you will receive me to glory.

25 Whom have I in heaven but you? And there is nothing on earth that I desire besides you.

26 My flesh and my heart may fail, but God is the strength of my heart and my portion forever.

27 For behold, those who are far from you shall perish; you put an end to everyone who is unfaithful to you.

28 But for me it is good to be near God; I have made the Lord God my refuge, that I may tell of all your works.

Like a speechless animal, I have been thinking that this physical life is everything. I have fallen into thinking the same way as people who ignore You. Since they think this is a dead-end world, they strive for riches, power, and fame. Even if they succeed in getting it all, they ask, "Is that all there is to life?" How disappointed they feel when everything turns to ashes in their hands.

No! This wonderful, beautiful physical life is only the beginning. While I am here, You walk hand in hand with me, guiding me along Your paths. When death separates me from this world, You will receive me into Your heavenly kingdom.

Why should I throw away Your loving kindness for worldly goods—cheap, shoddy substitutes for the dearest treasure? Please remind me that You are the strength of my heart when my body grows weary of working. When my spirit shrinks back from the test of doubt, remind me that You are my inheritance forever. Keep me steadfast and faithful. Give me opportunities to tell of Your goodness. Remind me that because of Your love I am a person of true wealth.

Psalm 74

1 O God, why do you cast us off forever? Why does your anger smoke against the sheep of your pasture?

2 Remember your congregation, which you have purchased of old, which you have redeemed to be the tribe of your heritage! Remember Mount Zion, where you have dwelt.

3 Direct your steps to the perpetual ruins; the enemy has destroyed everything in the sanctuary!

4 Your foes have roared in the midst of your meeting place; they set up their own signs for signs.

5 They were like those who swing axes in a forest of trees.

6 And all its carved wood they broke down with hatchets and hammers.

7 They set your sanctuary on fire; they profaned the dwelling place of your name, bringing it down to the ground.

8 They said to themselves, "We will utterly subdue them"; they burned all the meeting places of God in the land.

9 We do not see our signs; there is no longer any prophet, and there is none among us who knows how long.

10 How long, O God, is the foe to scoff? Is the enemy to revile your name forever?

11 Why do you hold back your hand, your right hand? Take it from the fold of your garment and destroy them!

12 Yet God my King is from of old, working salvation in the midst of the earth.

13 You divided the sea by your might; you broke the heads of the sea monsters on the waters.

Restrain the Tides of Evil

Lord, a tide of evil rushes upon us. Great tsunami waves seek to tear Your church completely off its Foundation. What's going on? Have You cast us off? You chose us to be born into Your kingdom. You bought us with the blood of Jesus Christ.

Remember the way we were before these evil times, Lord. Look at the endless ruins that now profane Your greatness. Take note of the internal sabotage and external attacks that Your church suffers. Lust and abuse of power by leaders within congregations flood Your church with adultery, homosexuality, and pedophilia. When confronted with their sins, these leaders fail to repent. They even proclaim their freedom to act as they please.

Thank you, Lord, that the majority of church leaders faithfully honor You. They courageously lead Your sheep to follow closely after You. However, if evil cannot sneak through the door, it will attempt to batter it down.

In China, government officials often bulldoze homes where congregations meet. In India, angry villagers sometimes burn churches while the congregation worships inside. In Iraq, Moslem extremists bomb churches. Everywhere in the world, Your enemies boast, "We will subdue these God-worshipers."

We search the Bible as the world grows more evil. We listen to those who speak Your Word, hoping to hear a promise of relief. Yet we find no comfortable platitude, only more cause for mourning. How long will You allow these riptides of evil to continue? Why do You restrain Your hand of protection?

You hold the power to destroy this evil tide. You are God, my King. You planned my salvation before You created the universe. You control the tides of time. By opening a dry road in the Red Sea, You saved the children of Israel and destroyed the Egyptians. You used the Greek and Roman civilizations to spread the good news of salvation through Jesus Christ. Their purpose served, they wasted away.

Nations have risen like springs of water and fallen like dried-up streams. Just as You set the boundaries of the earth and declared the flow of the seasons, so You have fixed boundaries upon the tides of evil and declared the day of their ending.

14 You crushed the heads of Leviathan; you gave him as food for the creatures of the wilderness.

15 You split open springs and brooks; you dried up ever-flowing streams.

16 Yours is the day, yours also the night; you have established the heavenly lights and the sun.

17 You have fixed all the boundaries of the earth; you have made summer and winter.

18 Remember this, O Lord, how the enemy scoffs, and a foolish people reviles your name.

19 Do not deliver the soul of your dove to the wild beasts; do not forget the life of your poor forever.

20 Have regard for the covenant, for the dark places of the land are full of the habitations of violence.

21 Let not the downtrodden turn back in shame; let the poor and needy praise your name.

22 Arise, O God, defend your cause; remember how the foolish scoff at you all the day!

23 Do not forget the clamor of your foes, the uproar of those who rise against you, which goes up continually!

Remember Your promise to keep us safe, even as we walk through the flood. Remember how the enemies scoff, how foolish people revile Your Name. Remind us that You inhabit the praises of Your people, even as we walk through the fire.

Now is a time of rising evil tides. Arise, oh God, to defend Your people. Make Your Name glorious. Restrain the clamor of Your foes and subdue those who rise against You. Let us rejoice in Your strong right hand.

Psalm 75

1 We give thanks to you, O God; we give thanks, for your name is near. We recount your wondrous deeds.

2 "At the set time that I appoint I will judge with equity.

3 When the earth totters, and all its inhabitants, it is I who keep steady its pillars.

Selah

4 I say to the boastful, 'Do not boast,' and to the wicked, 'Do not lift up your horn;

5 do not lift up your horn on high, or speak with haughty neck.'"

6 For not from the east or from the west and not from the wilderness comes lifting up,

7 but it is God who executes judgment, putting down one and lifting up another.

8 For in the hand of the Lord there is a cup with foaming wine, well mixed, and he pours out from it, and all the wicked of the earth shall drain it down to the dregs.

9 But I will declare it forever; I will sing praises to the God of Jacob.

10 All the horns of the wicked I will cut off, but the horns of the righteous shall be lifted up.

Humility or Humiliation

Father, forgive us. How can we act so wickedly? You saved us from our sins. You sent Your Spirit to live in our hearts. You bless us with Your presence and give us the wealth of Your kingdom. You give us opportunities to sing praises to You as we gather at church to worship.

Yet in our homes and in our hearts we boast of what we have. We proudly speak of our position and our possessions as if we obtained them by our own power. The stories we tell are about ourselves, not about the work You do in our lives.

You know the evil that still lurks in our hearts to trip us. We clutch tightly to everything we have exclaiming, "Mine! Mine!" While at the same time the Holy Spirit whispers, "Do not boast. Do not speak in your pride of your plans for the future. Turn away from this wickedness."

Father, in Your mercy, give us the power to reject the desire to live by our own strength. Open our eyes to see clearly the judgment coming on all our selfishness.

You judge our work to bring us to spiritual maturity. Your raise up those You can trust to obey and serve You. However, with those who serve themselves, You take away even what they have.

Father, teach us to surrender to You everything we have and all that we are. Give us the desire to live Your way instead of the way of this wicked world. Work in us the humility that we see in Jesus. Then You will lift us up in righteousness, not cast us down in humiliation. Then the praise we sing to You with our lips will echo in our hearts forever.

Psalm 76

1 In Judah God is known; his name is great in Israel.

2 His abode has been established in Salem, his dwelling place in Zion.

3 There he broke the flashing arrows, the shield, the sword, and the weapons of war.

Selah

4 Glorious are you, more majestic than the mountains of prey.

5 The stouthearted were stripped of their spoil; they sank into sleep; all the men of war were unable to use their hands.

6 At your rebuke, O God of Jacob, both rider and horse lay stunned.

7 But you, you are to be feared! Who can stand before you when once your anger is roused?

8 From the heavens you uttered judgment; the earth feared and was still,

9 when God arose to establish judgment, to save all the humble of the earth.

Selah

10 Surely the wrath of man shall praise you; the remnant of wrath you will put on like a belt.

11 Make your vows to the Lord your God and perform them; let all around him bring gifts to him who is to be feared,

12 who cuts off the spirit of princes, who is to be feared by the kings of the earth.

We Are Not the Judge

In Israel You are known, my God, but are You *known* in my country? Here Your Name is scorned and reviled. We use it more often in profanity than in prayer.

From all the places on earth, You established Jerusalem as the location for Your throne. (There You will rule all of humanity.) Historical accounts—from Joshua's time until the present—tell of Your divine protection of that city. You destroyed the weapons of war brought against them. Army after army melted away as they poured out their wrath against Your chosen people. At Your rebuke, enemy soldiers' hands hung limp and their hearts were stunned.

History is clear. The countries that work against Your purposes and fail to support Your people fall in destruction. Why then does our nation not fear You? Why do we doom ourselves to face Your judgment? If even the earth becomes quiet before Your wrath, why do we ignore You?

So often, we vent our frustration and bitterness against You. Even our indictments against You proclaim Your righteousness as You speak the verdict of "Guilty!" upon us. For our nation is not the judge but the accused.

Like Egypt long ago, we face the chaos of plagues. Even as the princes of that land defied You, so our leaders ignore Your warnings. Most of our leaders—from city mayors to president—believe their power comes from themselves alone. They do not acknowledge You or fear You.

Turn their arrogance to praise and their indifference to awe. Then shall they lead us to worship in Zion. Then shall Your wrath turn away from our land. Then shall we praise You instead of ignore You. Then shall our nation fulfill all Your plan.

Psalm 77

1 I cry aloud to God, aloud to God, and he will hear me.

2 In the day of my trouble I seek the Lord; in the night my hand is stretched out without wearying; my soul refuses to be comforted.

3 When I remember God, I moan; when I meditate, my spirit faints.

Selah

4 You hold my eyelids open; I am so troubled that I cannot speak.

5 I consider the days of old, the years long ago.

6 I said, "Let me remember my song in the night; let me meditate in my heart." Then my spirit made a diligent search:

7 "Will the Lord spurn forever, and never again be favorable?

8 Has his steadfast love forever ceased? Are his promises at an end for all time?

9 Has God forgotten to be gracious? Has he in anger shut up his compassion?"

Selah

10 Then I said, "I will appeal to this, to the years of the right hand of the Most High."

11 I will remember the deeds of the Lord; yes, I will remember your wonders of old.

12 I will ponder all your work, and meditate on your mighty deeds.

13 Your way, O God, is holy. What god is great like our God?

14 You are the God who works wonders; you have made known your might among the peoples.

Carry Me While I Cry

My baby! My baby is dead. Oh God, God, what can I do? How can I live through this? The unbearable pain flogs me. What happened? One day we lived an ordinary life with normal joys and pains. Then I heard, "Your child has died." Now I lie awake all night, my memory of this horrible thing repeating itself until my anguish exhausts me. I have cried and cried. Though my nose swelled shut and my eyes are raw, the tears fall.

God, how could You let this happen? You could have protected my baby. Are You punishing me?

I remember wonderful years: childish laughter, skinned knees, goodnight stories, and bedtime prayers. Now they are gone forever. My house echoes emptiness.

How can you say You will bless me when You took my baby? Has Your steadfast love failed me? You promised to work all things for my good, but how can taking my baby be good? Are You so angry with me that You cannot comfort me? Help me, Lord! Have pity on me. You watched Jesus die. Your Son was murdered. By His death I have forgiveness. Great good came from Jesus' death. I see no good coming from my child's death.

I know, Lord. You are The Holy One. Your ways are not my ways. My child was mine only for a season. How can any of that comfort me when my arms hang empty at my sides?

I feel battered, shattered by this brutal storm of pain—stricken by lightning, assaulted by thunderous peals, rain-torn and wind-tossed. Even anchored on the firm foundation of Your love, I feel the earth shake.

Your way leads through this flood? My path goes through this sea? Pain and sorrow blind me to the signposts of Your Way. Like a helpless little lamb, carry me while I cry.

15 You with your arm redeemed your people, the children of Jacob and Joseph.

Selah

16 When the waters saw you, O God, when the waters saw you, they were afraid; indeed, the deep trembled.

17 The clouds poured out water; the skies gave forth thunder; your arrows flashed on every side.

18 The crash of your thunder was in the whirlwind; your lightnings lighted up the world; the earth trembled and shook.

19 Your way was through the sea, your path through the great waters; yet your footprints were unseen.

20 You led your people like a flock by the hand of Moses and Aaron.

My Prayer

Psalm 78:1–8

1 Give ear, O my people, to my teaching; incline your ears to the words of my mouth!

2 I will open my mouth in a parable; I will utter dark sayings from of old,

3 things that we have heard and known, that our fathers have told us.

4 We will not hide them from their children, but tell to the coming generation the glorious deeds of the Lord, and his might, and the wonders that he has done.

5 He established a testimony in Jacob and appointed a law in Israel, which he commanded our fathers to teach to their children,

6 that the next generation might know them, the children yet unborn, and arise and tell them to their children,

7 so that they should set their hope in God and not forget the works of God, but keep his commandments;

8 and that they should not be like their fathers, a stubborn and rebellious generation, a generation whose heart was not steadfast, whose spirit was not faithful to God.

Like Links in a Chain

Father, I was reminded recently of a precious song I learned as a baby:
"Oh, be careful little lips what you say.
Oh, be careful little lips what you say.
For the Father up above
Is looking down in love,
So be careful little lips what you say."
I had not thought of that song in over half a century. Yet it continues to mold the words of my mouth.

I marvel when Your Spirit shows me how wonderfully You blessed me with godly parents. Before I could read or write, they taught me to love You. In simple songs and bedtime stories, I learned how much You love me. From mealtime prayers and Sunday school lessons, I learned that You give us the things we need and that You deserve our devotion.

Many of those who taught me to love You have died. Now I find myself responsible for teaching innocent little ones to know about You. What a privilege to tell the generation to come that You love them. I gladly introduce these babies to You, the God of creation. With every opportunity, I sing songs to them and teach them Your Word.

Father, send someone who follows You to each child at an age when their hearts are most receptive to You. Let them tell the children of Your love and of the wonders You perform. Use each of us to reach children who hunger for Your love.

You have ordained that each generation must transfer the Truth that it received to the generations coming after it. Like links in a chain, every generation must forge the ties between You and their children. How else can the children know of You and of how much You love them?

Father, by the power of Your Spirit because of the sacrifice of Your Son, let this be the generation who tells every child of the opportunity they have to be part of Your family. Reap a great harvest of tender young souls into Your kingdom. Overcome the failings of my generation—the failures of unprepared hearts and unfaithful spirits. Lead our children and grandchildren to set their hope in You.

Psalm 78:9–39

9 The Ephraimites, armed with the bow, turned back on the day of battle.

10 They did not keep God's covenant, but refused to walk according to his law.

11 They forgot his works and the wonders that he had shown them.

12 In the sight of their fathers he performed wonders in the land of Egypt, in the fields of Zoan.

13 He divided the sea and let them pass through it, and made the waters stand like a heap.

14 In the daytime he led them with a cloud, and all the night with a fiery light.

15 He split rocks in the wilderness and gave them drink abundantly as from the deep.

16 He made streams come out of the rock and caused waters to flow down like rivers.

17 Yet they sinned still more against him, rebelling against the Most High in the desert.

18 They tested God in their heart by demanding the food they craved.

19 They spoke against God, saying, "Can God spread a table in the wilderness?

20 He struck the rock so that water gushed out and streams overflowed. Can he also give bread or provide meat for his people?"

21 Therefore, when the Lord heard, he was full of wrath; a fire was kindled against Jacob; his anger rose against Israel,

As Fickle As the Wind

Lord, why do I always see what seems to be missing in life instead of seeing the full richness of the life You provide?

When I was spiritually mature enough to understand the seriousness of my actions, I committed to following You in every way, all the time. I thought I understood what that meant, but I didn't. Life went crazy wrong. My house filled with fear and the kitchen held no food to feed my children.

Did I turn to You in trust and ask, "What's next, Lord?" No, I began to challenge Your ability to care for us. My prayers were not about submission to Your will. I criticized You because the power was turned off. I didn't ask You to meet my needs, I bargained with You for the things I wanted—*"If You'll give me money to pay the rent, I'll stop complaining."*

Sure, I called You *Lord* with my lips and claimed that I trusted You. My heart told a different story. I filled it with resentment, blame, and bitterness. Humiliation added another layer of ugliness when our poverty-stricken neighbor fed us and I had to ask the property owner for extra time to pay the rent.

Occasionally, Your Spirit would reach through my fence of unbelief to comfort me. He would challenge me to trust You. I would shove my ugly feelings in a closet and slam the door, pushing myself to live out my commitment. Yet my efforts to keep it proved to be as fickle as the wind. It only took one child saying, "I don't want bread and peanut butter, again," for the closet door to burst open and all of those emotions to swirl through my heart.

Were You angry to see my fickle ways? I know I would be frustrated to see someone fail every test. Yes, every opportunity I had to trust You, I failed.

Why did I not thank You that the owner of the house was willing to wait for the rent, that we never went one day without food, and that You sent people to help us through the crisis? Instead of submitting, I rebelled in my pride. I did all that I could to get through the crisis without help and it wasn't enough.

Finally, my pride collapsed and my misplaced confidence in my ability to provide died. Finally, my lips, my mind, and my heart all agreed: Your way is best. Your way is the *only* way. When I focused on You, You showed

22 because they did not believe in God and did not trust his saving power.

23 Yet he commanded the skies above and opened the doors of heaven,

24 and he rained down on them manna to eat and gave them the grain of heaven.

25 Man ate of the bread of the angels; he sent them food in abundance.

26 He caused the east wind to blow in the heavens, and by his power he led out the south wind;

27 he rained meat on them like dust, winged birds like the sand of the seas;

28 he let them fall in the midst of their camp, all around their dwellings.

29 And they ate and were well filled, for he gave them what they craved.

30 But before they had satisfied their craving, while the food was still in their mouths,

31 the anger of God rose against them, and he killed the strongest of them and laid low the young men of Israel.

32 In spite of all this, they still sinned; despite his wonders, they did not believe.

33 So he made their days vanish like a breath, and their years in terror.

34 When he killed them, they sought him; they repented and sought God earnestly.

35 They remembered that God was their rock, the Most High God their redeemer.

me compassion and forgave me. My anger, bitterness, and resentment drained away and I was able to sleep again.

I wish that were the only time You and I had to deal with my fickleness. Unfortunately, it pops up, usually when I least expect it. You know that about me. You also know that my commitment to follow You is sincere. However, I just do not always obey You as I wish I did.

Thank You for remembering that I waver sometimes like a puff of wind. Thank You for picking me up, giving me a hug, and setting me back on my feet. Thank You for patiently leading me forward in the life that You have planned.

36 But they flattered him with their mouths; they lied to him with their tongues.

37 Their heart was not steadfast toward him; they were not faithful to his covenant.

38 Yet he, being compassionate, atoned for their iniquity and did not destroy them; he restrained his anger often and did not stir up all his wrath.

39 He remembered that they were but flesh, a wind that passes and comes not again.

MY PRAYER

Psalm 78:40–55

40 How often they rebelled against him in the wilderness and grieved him in the desert!

41 They tested God again and again and provoked the Holy One of Israel.

42 They did not remember his power or the day when he redeemed them from the foe,

43 when he performed his signs in Egypt and his marvels in the fields of Zoan.

44 He turned their rivers to blood, so that they could not drink of their streams.

45 He sent among them swarms of flies, which devoured them, and frogs, which destroyed them.

46 He gave their crops to the destroying locust and the fruit of their labor to the locust.

47 He destroyed their vines with hail and their sycamores with frost.

48 He gave over their cattle to the hail and their flocks to thunderbolts.

49 He let loose on them his burning anger, wrath, indignation, and distress, a company of destroying angels.

50 He made a path for his anger; he did not spare them from death, but gave their lives over to the plague.

51 He struck down every firstborn in Egypt, the first fruits of their strength in the tents of Ham.

52 Then he led out his people like sheep and guided them in the wilderness like a flock.

Living in the Foggy Middle

Lord, as I read the account of the Israelites' rebellion and unbelief, it occurs to me that their story and mine have much in common. In Egypt, they lived in a culture where Your Name was not honored. They were slaves who were part of an idolatrous society. What little they knew about You came from the stories passed down in their families for 400 years. No spiritual desire to know You existed in them. You heard only their groaning under their burden of life.

Yet You gave to this huge extended family Your favor, which they neither sought nor deserved. They were in the middle of a story that began with a promise to Abraham. They didn't know that You had them driven out of Egypt for a reason. They didn't understand that they would inherit the land given by You to Abraham. They saw "natural disasters" instead of Your wrath sent to break the power of a mighty pagan nation.

Once they left Egypt, no extraordinary change in the attitudes of the Israelites occurred. Their grumbling and complaining erupted many times into outright rebellion. Often, they wanted to return to Egypt.

In the middle of their unbelief, You continued to pour out favor they didn't deserve. You provided food and water in the desert. For forty years, their shoes and clothes did not wear out. You turned shepherd-slaves into an army that won impressive victories on both sides of the Jordan River.

In spite of all of the Israelites' rebellion and unbelief, Abraham's faith produced fruit for his children. You kept Your promise to him. You planted his family in the Promised Land.

Lord, I live in an idolatrous culture, too. Many times, I am a slave to society's whims. My bad attitude can keep me from seeing Your hand at work in the events of my life. I live in the foggy middle of the story. I cannot see how the changes and problems I face further Your plan for my life.

I know from the things You tell me in the Bible that I live every day in the center of Your unmerited favor. Open my eyes to see it. Teach me to recognize and appreciate Your favor. Move my heart and train my mind so that I work with You instead of complaining.

53 He led them in safety, so that they were not afraid, but the sea overwhelmed their enemies.

54 And he brought them to his holy land, to the mountain which his right hand had won.

55 He drove out nations before them; he apportioned them for a possession and settled the tribes of Israel in their tents.

Just because my situation is similar to the Israelites' doesn't mean that I must react the way they did. My desire is to respond to Your favor with obedience and to Your actions with faith. Let the way I respond to Your will for my life bring glory to Your Name, not pain to Your heart.

Psalm 78:56–66

56 Yet they tested and rebelled against the Most High God and did not keep his testimonies,

57 but turned away and acted treacherously like their fathers; they twisted like a deceitful bow.

58 For they provoked him to anger with their high places; they moved him to jealousy with their idols.

59 When God heard, he was full of wrath, and he utterly rejected Israel.

60 He forsook his dwelling at Shiloh, the tent where he dwelt among mankind,

61 and delivered his power to captivity, his glory to the hand of the foe.

62 He gave his people over to the sword and vented his wrath on his heritage.

63 Fire devoured their young men, and their young women had no marriage song.

64 Their priests fell by the sword, and their widows made no lamentation.

65 Then the Lord awoke as from sleep, like a strong man shouting because of wine.

66 And he put his adversaries to rout; he put them to everlasting shame.

Patient Love for Wayward Man

Lord, is it any wonder that You become angry with the people You love? You pour out sunshine and rain, food and prosperity, safety and peace. Some people praise You, obey You, and joyfully share Your bounty. Yet others—in the same circumstances—use Your blessings to make false gods of greed, pride, and entitlement.

These "self-made" people think that hard work and "luck" bring them the positions and wealth they "deserve." They arrogantly attribute everything good in their lives to anything other than You—The Only Source. They fix their attention on these other things and worship them.

You place people in their lives to show them the truth and to give them Your love. Yet they continue to reject Your message. They talk instead about "mother nature" and "many ways to god." They provoke You to anger and move You to jealousy.

In Your anger, You give them the things they deserve: illness strikes, accident cripples, wealth evaporates, peace shatters. Yet even Your anger is an expression of Your love. Your intention is to bring people to repentance, not destruction. Your anger drives some people back to You. They abandon their false gods and seek You with their whole hearts.

How You must rejoice to see people free of their slavery to these "gods." You delight in giving Yourself to them, replacing their feelings of abandonment with a sense of completion and fulfillment. They respond to Your love and are accepted in the Beloved.

Nevertheless, some people respond to Your anger with resentment and renewed rejection. "I can't believe in a god who does such bad things to good people," they say. No expression of Your love finds an answering response in their hearts.

Once more, You warn them of the consequences of their rebellion. Your message this time is that if they choose to remain Your adversaries, then they will face Your judgment. You will put them to everlasting shame. You always give them one final opportunity to choose to repent.

Your patient love for wayward man is forever worthy of praise.

Psalm 78:67–72

67 He rejected the tent of Joseph; he did not choose the tribe of Ephraim,

68 but he chose the tribe of Judah, Mount Zion, which he loves.

69 He built his sanctuary like the high heavens, like the earth, which he has founded forever.

70 He chose David his servant and took him from the sheepfolds;

71 from following the nursing ewes he brought him to shepherd Jacob his people, Israel his inheritance.

72 With upright heart he shepherded them and guided them with his skillful hand.

To Be Chosen

My Lord, You are The One Who Chooses.

You chose Joseph to become the means by which You saved his family from famine. He faithfully followed You. Yet hundreds of years later, You rejected the tribe descended from his son, Ephraim. Was it because they had become arrogant and selfish?

Instead, You chose a descendent of Judah. Judah was one of Joseph's older brothers, a man careless about keeping his promise and the father of sinful sons. Certainly, nothing would recommend this man's family.

Outwardly, nothing would recommend his descendent David, either. He was the youngest son of an unimportant family. Unlike Joseph, who was his father's pampered favorite, David was sent out alone with the sheep.

When You had him anointed as king of Israel, he lived at the sheep pens, caring for the pregnant ewes and baby lambs. He spent his time wrestling with silly mama sheep that wouldn't let their lambs nurse. It was a dirty, endless job with little time for David to rest.

You were the only one who knew that caring for ewes in the sheep pens and leading the flocks in the fields were part of "king training." Hidden in David's heart was a dynamic dependence on You. Those many lonely hours were busy seasons of preparation. You were growing David's faith.

Though You anointed David to be king as a young man, many years of struggle followed his anointing. Then, just as You had planned, he was crowned king of Israel. He ruled Israel with integrity and skill, just as You had intended.

From the beginning of David's life, You made choices for him. You chose a hardworking family with critical older brothers. You chose a lonely childhood out in the hills where he learned to lead and protect the flocks of sheep. You chose years where he lived as a fugitive, running from King Saul. You chose him to be the servant-king over Israel. You chose him to be an ancestor of Jesus Christ, Your only begotten Son.

David didn't know, as he led the sheep, that You had chosen him. Neither do I know, as I go through my daily activities, what You have chosen for me to accomplish. This one thing I do know: I want nothing in me to cause You to reject me as You rejected the tribe of Ephraim. Instead,

My Prayer

I want to work diligently in my ordinary days, looking for ways to show Your love. I will bloom where You have planted me.

I know that my attitude and actions—today—prepare me to be either chosen or rejected for You to use tomorrow. Work in me, my Lord, so that I am always Your useful servant. May the skills I learn in this season of my life bring You glory in the next season. Choose me, Lord.

Psalm 79

1. O God, the nations have come into your inheritance; they have defiled your holy temple; they have laid Jerusalem in ruins.

2. They have given the bodies of your servants to the birds of the heavens for food, the flesh of your faithful to the beasts of the earth.

3. They have poured out their blood like water all around Jerusalem, and there was no one to bury them.

4. We have become a taunt to our neighbors, mocked and derided by those around us.

5. How long, O Lord? Will you be angry forever? Will your jealousy burn like fire?

6. Pour out your anger on the nations that do not know you, and on the kingdoms that do not call upon your name!

7. For they have devoured Jacob and laid waste his habitation.

8. Do not remember against us our former iniquities; let your compassion come speedily to meet us, for we are brought very low.

9. Help us, O God of our salvation, for the glory of your name; deliver us, and atone for our sins, for your name's sake!

10. Why should the nations say, "Where is their God?" Let the avenging of the outpoured blood of your servants be known among the nations before our eyes!

11. Let the groans of the prisoners come before you; according to your great power, preserve those doomed to die!

12. Return sevenfold into the lap of our neighbors the taunts with which they have taunted you, O Lord!

13. But we your people, the sheep of your pasture, will give thanks to you forever; from generation to generation we will recount your praise.

Where Were You, God?

The ruins of the city coated in blood. Corpses filling the fields, a harvest of rotting flesh.

Where were You, God, when pagan soldiers destroyed Jerusalem and defiled Your Temple?

So many times Your prophets had warned Your people, "Don't worship false gods. God demands your complete loyalty. Idol worship brings God's punishment."

So many times their shallow repentance became the doorway to more callous rejection of You and increased worship of idols. They traded purity and peace with You for depravity and fear of the demons that the idols represented.

You were like a parent with a disobedient child who ignores repeated warnings and throws off milder forms of punishment. You displayed Your love and passionate commitment to the nation of Israel when You put their good above Your own reputation. You saw that it would take extreme measures to remove Your people from the road of destruction.

Where were You? You were right there, pouring out this cup of wrath upon Your chosen nation. They had been impervious to every other expression of Your merciful love. Nevertheless, You would not let this nation destroy itself with idolatry. Your mercy and compassion did not fail. It came in the form of an overwhelming invading army.

This time the people of Israel got Your message. They suffered exile from the Promised Land, but You returned their children and grandchildren. They rebuilt the Temple and the city of Jerusalem. Never again did Israel reject You for false gods.

Lord Jesus, I know that You are passionately committed to Your bride, the church. Your commitment to Your bride's purity is no less than Jehovah's commitment to the nation of Israel. You guard us against the filth and immorality of this world. Keep our pastors and other leaders sensitive to Your voice so that You need not take extreme measures to protect us from waywardness. Give each member of every congregation a heart that heeds the Words of Life. Give each of us a spirit of humility so that we willingly follow You. Then the world will see that our good is found only in Your glory. Then Your people will give You thanks and bless Your Name forever.

Psalm 80

1. Give ear, O Shepherd of Israel, you who lead Joseph like a flock! You who are enthroned upon the cherubim, shine forth.

2. Before Ephraim and Benjamin and Manasseh, stir up your might and come to save us!

3. Restore us, O God; let your face shine, that we may be saved!

4. O Lord God of hosts, how long will you be angry with your people's prayers?

5. You have fed them with the bread of tears and given them tears to drink in full measure.

6. You make us an object of contention for our neighbors, and our enemies laugh among themselves.

7. Restore us, O God of hosts; let your face shine, that we may be saved!

8. You brought a vine out of Egypt; you drove out the nations and planted it.

9. You cleared the ground for it; it took deep root and filled the land.

10. The mountains were covered with its shade, the mighty cedars with its branches.

11. It sent out its branches to the sea and its shoots to the River.

12. Why then have you broken down its walls, so that all who pass along the way pluck its fruit?

13. The boar from the forest ravages it, and all that move in the field feed on it.

The Saving Shepherd

Oh God, Father of Your chosen ones, stir up Your might and come to our rescue.

Like sheep that pay attention to nothing beyond reaching that next bite of grass, we get ourselves stranded in impossible places when we stray from Your side. Do you roll Your eyes and shake Your head as You watch us rush into the brambles for that tempting tidbit? Hoping that we will learn our lesson about straying from You, do you allow us to be caught in the thorny bushes of sin?

We thrash around, confining ourselves more completely until we can no longer move. Then we cry, "Rescue us, Lord, save us! Get us out of this mess." You gently free us from the trap that snares us.

Yet many times the lesson we learn is not, "Stay close to God so You'll be safe from temptation." Silly sheep that we are, the lesson we learn is, "It doesn't matter what we do, God won't let us get hurt." How can You be so patient with us?

Armed with this false confidence, we stray farther next time. We ramble over the hill and into the wilderness. There, thieves catch us. They fight over who will keep us, pulling us one way and then another. When they hear a pack of wild dogs, they drop us and flee, leaving us to be the prey of hungry animals. Lost and panic stricken, we cry out for you to rescue us. Do our tears wash away Your righteous anger? Again, You restore us to Your side.

For a third time we stray from You. Instead of following You to streams of quiet water, we go down to the mud-filled watering hole. Before we can drink from the sin-polluted pond, the mud has sucked us deeply into the mire. Filthy mud drags us down, flies torment us, and wild dogs struggle to pull us out for food.

We have come to the end of our own strength. Only You can save us. We call out to You, "Let Your hand give us life and we shall not turn back from You. Rescue us, Oh Lord God of hosts. Restore us to Your side that we may be saved." And You come.

14 Turn again, O God of hosts! Look down from heaven, and see; have regard for this vine,

15 the stock that your right hand planted, and for the son whom you made strong for yourself.

16 They have burned it with fire; they have cut it down; may they perish at the rebuke of your face!

17 But let your hand be on the man of your right hand, the son of man whom you have made strong for yourself!

18 Then we shall not turn back from you; give us life, and we will call upon your name!

19 Restore us, O Lord God of hosts! let your face shine, that we may be saved!

My Prayer

Psalm 81

1 Sing aloud to God our strength; shout for joy to the God of Jacob!

2 Raise a song; sound the tambourine, the sweet lyre with the harp.

3 Blow the trumpet at the new moon, at the full moon, on our feast day.

4 For it is a statute for Israel, a rule of the God of Jacob.

5 He made it a decree in Joseph when he went out over the land of Egypt. I hear a language I had not known:

6 "I relieved your shoulder of the burden; your hands were freed from the basket.

7 In distress you called, and I delivered you; I answered you in the secret place of thunder; I tested you at the waters of Meribah.

Selah

8 Hear, O my people, while I admonish you! O Israel, if you would but listen to me!

9 There shall be no strange god among you; you shall not bow down to a foreign god.

10 I am the Lord your God, who brought you up out of the land of Egypt. Open your mouth wide, and I will fill it.

11 "But my people did not listen to my voice; Israel would not submit to me.

12 So I gave them over to their stubborn hearts, to follow their own counsels.

13 Oh, that my people would listen to me, that Israel would walk in my ways!

Songs of Worship

Lord God, when we join our voices together on Sunday morning to worship You with songs of praise, how my heart rises in joyful celebration. Every fiber of my being acclaims Your worthiness. Hearing all the voices rising in praise around me incites me to higher levels of exultation. My joy and enthusiasm swallow all my cares and burdens. My heart and mind are captured by the words we sing in worship of Your holiness.

Yet after I leave the church, sometimes I get no farther than the parking lot before my spirit of praise pops like an over-filled balloon. The cares of my life rush in to replace my thoughts of You. My worship is short-lived.

However, Your Word tells me that You are my God every day of the week, not just on Sunday morning. Emotions that change like the tides are no excuse for living my life most days of the week as if You do not exist. You desire that I seek Your will and obey it every day. When I replace worship with worry and praise with fear, I reveal the idols I worship.

Please God, do not give me up to my own ways. Transform my stubborn heart. It keeps insisting that You don't understand. Change it into a heart that follows You even if it doesn't understand. Show me how to be a God-follower every day.

What precious gifts You promise to give me as I follow You day by day: the finest bread of Your presence and the sweetness of Your fellowship. Teach me to desire Your presence and fellowship so that I am completely dissatisfied without that experience every day. Give me songs for worship every day.

14 I would soon subdue their enemies and turn my hand against their foes.

15 Those who hate the Lord would cringe toward him, and their fate would last forever.

16 But he would feed you with the finest of the wheat, and with honey from the rock I would satisfy you."

My Prayer

Psalm 82

1. God has taken his place in the divine council; in the midst of the gods he holds judgment:

2. "How long will you judge unjustly and show partiality to the wicked?

   Selah

3. Give justice to the weak and the fatherless; maintain the right of the afflicted and the destitute.

4. Rescue the weak and the needy; deliver them from the hand of the wicked."

5. They have neither knowledge nor understanding, they walk about in darkness; all the foundations of the earth are shaken.

6. I said, "You are gods, sons of the Most High, all of you;

7. nevertheless, like men you shall die, and fall like any prince."

8. Arise, O God, judge the earth; for you shall inherit all the nations!

The Supreme Court

Father, one of Your great gifts to us is the rule of law. You gave us moral laws in the Bible and from them we write laws for our society. By the laws, we declare which behavior is acceptable and which is not. You give us laws for peace and stability. Thank You for this wonderful gift.

Yet because we are rebellious humanity, we disagree over the interpretation of the laws as soon as we write them. Because we are sinful, You appoint judges, giving them part of your own responsibility. In that respect, they become "gods."

Down through the ages, You have held judges accountable for maintaining justice. You confront them with their partiality when they fail. You challenge them about their ignorance of Your ways and their arrogance. So many people who want to become judges do not understand that You judge the judges. Let Your Word warn and instruct them.

Lord, give us judges who trust in You. Give us men and women who understand that they represent You when they decide questions of law and of punishment. Give them wisdom greater than Solomon's and the ability to communicate clearly. Protect them from temptation and from threats. Sustain them so that they do not become weary in doing well or frustrated by their limitations.

Above all, Lord God Almighty, remind judges that You will review every decision they make. On the day You begin to reign over the nations, You will convene the Supreme Court of all the earth and judge the judges.

Psalm 83

1 O God, do not keep silence; do not hold your peace or be still, O God!

2 For behold, your enemies make an uproar; those who hate you have raised their heads.

3 They lay crafty plans against your people; they consult together against your treasured ones.

4 They say, "Come, let us wipe them out as a nation; let the name of Israel be remembered no more!"

5 For they conspire with one accord; against you they make a covenant—

6 the tents of Edom and the Ishmaelites, Moab and the Hagrites,

7 Gebal and Ammon and Amalek, Philistia with the inhabitants of Tyre;

8 Asshur also has joined them; they are the strong arm of the children of Lot.

Selah

9 Do to them as you did to Midian, as to Sisera and Jabin at the river Kishon,

10 who were destroyed at En-dor, who became dung for the ground.

11 Make their nobles like Oreb and Zeeb, all their princes like Zebah and Zalmunna,

12 who said, "Let us take possession for ourselves of the pastures of God."

13 O my God, make them like whirling dust, like chaff before the wind.

Your Purpose Stands

Father, in every generation the wicked lead the way in opposing Your purpose and in oppressing those who love You. In the time when Psalm 83 was written, wicked rulers threatened to overthrow Israel and to destroy it. They opposed the people You chose to own the Promised Land. Flash forward and today the picture is much the same; wicked leaders obsess over destroying the nation of Israel. They seek to erase Your people in The Land, just as in the time of Israel's kings.

Your Word records many accounts of times when You rescued Your people from enemies who attacked them in overwhelming numbers. The Bible also informs us that—at other times—You used their enemies to punish Israel for turning away from You and worshipping idols. Nevertheless, wicked leaders never succeeded in destroying Your people. Praise Your Name, Your purpose stands forever!

Now as then, oh Lord, protect Your people for Your Name's sake. By the power of Your might, bring the wicked leaders to their knees. Show them their powerlessness to thwart Your purpose. Cause them to confess that You are God and that the land and the people of Israel belong to You. More than that, bring repentance to their hearts and confession to their lips as they embrace Jesus as Savior and Lord. Let the miracle of wicked leaders becoming part of Your kingdom spark a world-encompassing wildfire of people repenting before You. Display to the world that Your purpose stands forever.

14 As fire consumes the forest, as the flame sets the mountains ablaze,

15 so may you pursue them with your tempest and terrify them with your hurricane!

16 Fill their faces with shame, that they may seek your name, O Lord.

17 Let them be put to shame and dismayed forever; let them perish in disgrace,

18 that they may know that you alone, whose name is the Lord, are the Most High over all the earth.

My Prayer

CPSIA information can be obtained at www.ICGtesting.com
Printed in the USA
LVOW062013280911

248260LV00002B/3/P